Scotland Yard

Sir Harold Scott
GCVO, KCB, KBE

Commissioner of the Metropolitan Police
1945–53

A Mayflower Paperback

SCOTLAND YARD
Sir Harold Scott

Copyright Sir Harold Scott 1954

First published by André Deutsch Ltd. 1954

Published as a Mayflower Paperback 1970

TO
THE MEN AND WOMEN
OF THE
METROPOLITAN POLICE

Mayflower Paperbacks are published by
Mayflower Books,
3 Upper James Street, London, W.1.
Made and printed in Great Britain by
Hunt Barnard & Co. Ltd., Aylesbury, Bucks.

Contents

1 Introduction to Scotland Yard 7
2 Post-war Crime 11
3 Young Men in Trouble 23
4 The Police, the Press, and the Public 37
5 The Haigh Case 54
6 The Criminal Investigation Department 64
7 The Criminal Record Office 76
8 The Fingerprint Department 84
9 The Forensic Science Laboratory 93
10 Christie 102
11 The Flying Squad 111
12 The Fraud Squad 125
13 The Black Museum 129
14 The Special Branch and the Visit of
    Marshal Tito 136
15 The Stone of Scone 146
16 The Thames Division 158
17 The Women Police 162
18 The Mounted Police and the Dogs 168
19 The Problems of London's Traffic 175
20 Great Occasions 181

Chapter 1

INTRODUCTION TO SCOTLAND YARD

ONE day towards the end of 1944 I received an invitation from Mr Herbert Morrison, the Home Secretary, to visit him at the Home Office.

At that time I was Permanent Secretary of the Ministry of Aircraft Production and busily engaged with Sir Stafford Cripps and the Chief Executive, Air Chief Marshal Sir Wilfrid Freeman, in the problems of supplying and maintaining the vast numbers of aircraft needed by the R.A.F. in Europe and the Far East. This and post-war plans for jet-engines and other things made M.A.P. a busy and absorbing job and I had no thought of leaving it. Having worked with Mr Morrison during the early years of the war at the Ministry of Home Security, I went to the Home Office expecting that our talk would be on some aspect of Civil Defence.

Mr Morrison, who had a sense of humour, may have been aware of what was in my mind and wished to take me by surprise, for one of his first questions was 'Can you ride a horse?' Somewhat disconcerted, I replied that I had never been much of a horseman and had not ridden for many years; but I said I had no doubt I could ride well enough not to disgrace myself.

The Home Secretary then invited me to accept after the war the position of Commissioner of Police of the Metropolis.

To say that I was astonished would be an understatement. The first joint Commissioners of Police of the Metropolis in 1829 were Sir Richard Mayne, a lawyer, and Colonel Sir Charles Rowan, an army officer. Since that time it had become almost traditional for the Commissioner to be chosen from among senior officers of the armed forces, and it was expected that when the then Commissioner, Air Vice Marshal Sir Philip Game, retired, tradition would be followed.

But Mr Morrison had his own ideas. He wished to emphasise the civilian character of the police force and thought that in the changed conditions of a post-war world the work of the Commissioner would call rather for experience of administra-

7

tion in a big civil department than experience in the military field. He was good enough to say that as a result of our association for three years in Civil Defence he thought I could do the job.

I was less sure. It was true that though when I went to the Ministry of Aircraft Production I knew little about aircraft or the language of the R.A.F., I had found that once one learned the language, the problems, though in a new field, called for similar judgements of men and facts as in my earlier experience.

It was true also that I had begun my Civil Service career in 1911 in that department of the Home Office which dealt with the Metropolitan Police, and as chairman of the Prison Commissioners for seven years I had seen, as it were, the end product of police work. But I could not help wondering how a Civil Service chief would be viewed by the men of the biggest police force in this country. The public, too, expecting discipline from the police, might have their confidence shaken by a civilian appointment.

If these doubts could be overcome, however, I found the proposal attractive. It was a chance to escape from the burden of paperwork which bears ever more heavily on the high officials of Whitehall and to deal direct with men and their problems. At the Prison Commission, I had found in the personal relations and problems of that service an interest and satisfaction which had been lacking in my earlier departmental work. I felt sure that I should find the work of the Metropolitan Police equally interesting, and from the point of view of public service the work was obviously important.

Thinking, perhaps, of the new war in terms of the old, I anticipated at that time that the war would be followed by a period of rapid change and readjustment. There would be more crime; not only violent crime which is always a comparatively small part of the whole, but the petty dishonesty – burglary, fraud or larceny in various forms – which is the main burden of police work.

This had been the pattern after the first world war, when there had also been considerable industrial unrest which might be repeated. Whatever government was in power, its plans of social reform must be allowed to develop and outgrow their teething troubles in an atmosphere of calm and good order. For this the country would look to the police and on their loyalty and efficiency much would depend. Could a civilian hope to secure the discipline which the public and government would expect?

As chairman of the Prison Commission I had been greatly influenced by the late Sir Alexander Paterson, to whose practical idealism our penal system owes so much. We had worked closely together on Lord Templewood's Criminal Justice Bill which was an early war casualty, and together we had launched the open Borstal institutions at North Sea Camp, Hollesley Bay and Usk, and the prison camp near Wakefield which was the forerunner of several similar prison camps opened since the war.

Discipline, Paterson never wearied of saying, depends on leadership rather than repression. Given fair treatment, recognition of merit and avoidance of favouritism, discipline will follow as a matter of course. In our work together we had learned by experience the value of these principles, and it was with this in mind that I considered the problem of discipline in the police force.

I had come to know the police well during the days and nights of the blitz on London, and to admire their helpfulness and sense of duty in an emergency. Discipline in the police and in the armed forces, it seemed to me, were different things. Military discipline trains men to do in a body, automatically and under stress, what they have been taught to do in times of peace. The police rarely act as a body. The policeman is almost always alone, and must make up his own mind to a course of action which cannot always be covered by the most comprehensive general order.

A car thief, possibly armed and desperate, bolts down a dark alley. No one will be the wiser if the policeman chasing him returns to the station and reports that the man got away. But the free discipline of the police, the pride in their job, is such that they will follow the man into the unknown, unarmed themselves except for their truncheon, facing possible disablement or death. It was this kind of discipline which I had to encourage.

I put aside my doubts, therefore, and told Mr Morrison I would be glad and proud to undertake the work which he offered. It was arranged that I should succeed Sir Philip Game on June 1, 1945, and so, immediately after the collapse of Germany, having received the Royal Warrant, I was summoned to Buckingham Palace and shown into His Majesty's large study. He invited me to sit down beside the fire and after some talk about my earlier work in the Prison Commission and elsewhere, he spoke about the work of the Metropolitan Police and how helpful the officers attached to the Palace had always been. He foresaw the heavy problems of crime and traffic that lay ahead, and ended by wishing me good luck in the new task I was undertaking.

A few days later, my wife and I went round to the Lord Chancellor's chambers overlooking Victoria Tower gardens, where we listened to an impromptu discourse by the late Lord Simon on the office of the Commissioner of Police. Then without ceremony, as is the British way, I took the oath before him undertaking to carry out my duties faithfully and loyally to the Crown, and so entered upon my work at Scotland Yard.

The Commissioner's Office is a large corner room, comfortably furnished with leather chairs and an open fire, on the first floor overlooking the Thames just below Westminster Bridge. The room was a war casualty, for on May 11, 1941, a high explosive bomb scored a hit immediately above it and brought a mass of masonry and rubble, and a huge card index, on to the Commissioner's desk. The room was empty at the time and Sir Philip Game arrived half an hour later to find his room a complete wreck. Repairs were started at once. They cost over £22,000, and as a result I inherited what it pleased me to call the newest government office in London.

One day in my first week as I entered my room, I found about a dozen chairs arranged in a semi-circle before my desk. I asked what they were for, and was told that they were for my first weekly conference with my senior officers and that this had always been the arrangement of such conferences in the past. I immediately said that I did not propose to address my colleagues as if I were a schoolmaster in front of his class, and had the chairs rearranged round a table. When my senior officers saw the new arrangement, their faces wore a look of startled surmise, but the new plan had the effect I intended and from then onward our conferences became friendly and informal talks at which everyone felt free to speak his mind on any subject that came up.

It was a small matter, but symbolic of my aim, that everyone should work as a member of a team in the tasks that lay ahead.

Chapter 2
POST-WAR CRIME

In his first instruction to the newly formed Metropolitan Police, Sir Richard Mayne said that the absence of crime would be the truest evidence of the efficiency of the Force. Judged by this standard, the Metropolitan Police, and indeed every force in the country, can derive little satisfaction from the crime statistics of the post-war years. But an examination of the causes and the statistics of crime since 1945 is worthwhile if only to demonstrate that, serious as the figures are, they are not in themselves evidence of any lack of skill or keenness on the part of a depleted force, who have indeed faced an almost insuperable task with courage and ingenuity.

It is always said that an increase in crime is the inevitable aftermath of every great war, and experience after the first world war certainly lent support to this saying. After an even longer and more devastating second war the police were under no illusions about the problems they would have to contend with.

War at any time is not calculated to foster a respect for life and property, and a war to the death like the last one, in which the State perforce made great inroads on the liberties of the subject and the rights of property, was hardly the school in which one could expect respect for the law and the rights of others to flourish.

The war, too, brought into being innumerable restrictions which, however necessary to the war effort, were not always so obviously necessary to the man in the street. He did not regard an evasion of these restrictions as carrying with it the same moral stigma as crime in the old sense, and so there arose a lack of respect for the law which gradually spread to wider fields.

The war itself took a form hitherto unknown. Thousands of people were uprooted from their usual surroundings. Evacuation of women, children and old people, sometimes two or three times repeated, landed them in strange places among new

11

people and unknown ways of life. The children suffered especially. Hundreds of thousands were deprived of the feelings of stability and security so necessary to the development of the young mind. After the war, it was not surprising to find among these children, now grown to adolescence, a large proportion of the offenders that came before the courts.

Apart from the moral and social effects of war, the black out and the material damage caused by air raids combined to place unusual temptations in the way of young people. Thousands of damaged doors and windows which were only repaired temporarily, offered a wonderful opportunity for picking and stealing. And when young offenders were caught, the Probation Service, Approved Schools and Borstal Institutions had to deal with them with sadly depleted staff, for they had given up many of their youngest and best men to the fighting forces. To those who remained it was a disheartening struggle to cope with the great number of young people committed to their charge.

It has sometimes been suggested that the training of millions of young men to war was in itself calculated to lead them to employ violence on their return to civilian life. Commando training was often singled out for special opprobrium on this ground, but the suggestions never seemed to me to have any real foundation.

The Commandos were, in fact, trained to a high degree of self-discipline and self-reliance, with a grim purpose which they well understood and accepted; and neither they nor the ordinary members of the armed forces – which, be it remembered, represented a large part of our young men and women – gave any solid reason for this thoughtless libel. The police found nothing in their experience to support it.

But while it would be unfair to saddle the armed forces with responsibility for the increase in crimes of violence, the same cannot be said of crimes of dishonesty. War is necessarily wasteful and those who take part in it have always felt themselves absolved to some extent from respect for property. They take as they need, and though taking is euphemistically described as 'winning' or 'finding', the scrounger is in fact a thief. Some, unfortunately, have brought back to civil life the habits acquired in the Services. It is not surprising, therefore, that after the war crimes of dishonesty rose to a new high level.

Another class often blamed for the post-war increase in

crime was that of the deserters. There were many thousands of these, and some undoubtedly found it difficult to settle quietly into civil life. On the run, without ration or identity cards which had become part of our modern equipment, they found it hard to earn a living in the ordinary way and took to crime as a temporary solution of their problems. But their share in the crime figures has often been exaggerated. The dangerous criminal in fact found little difficulty in equipping himself with all the documents he needed, while a large part of post-war crime has been the work, not of deserters, but of men too young to have served in the war.

Crime in English law is divided into two main groups – indictable and non-indictable. The first group includes all those more serious offences which may be tried on indictment – that is, before a Judge and Jury, either at Quarter Sessions or at Assizes. They are not always so tried; for with the consent of the accused many of them may be tried by a court of summary jurisdiction, i.e. a Stipendiary Magistrate or a Bench of Justices. But however tried, these offences appear in the statistics as indictable crimes and include a wide variety of offences from stealing sixpence to murder.

Non-indictable offences are all dealt with summarily, and include such offences as drunkenness, breach of local by-laws or government regulations and minor traffic offences. In general, they are less serious and less heinous than indictable offences, and often denote carelessness, or even bad luck rather than criminal intent; though such offences as dangerous driving can hardly be so regarded.

Statistics of indictable offences, therefore, make a very good index of the state of crime, and it is to these we generally refer when speaking of the subject.

Strictly comparable figures do not go back beyond 1933, when Lord Trenchard introduced a new system of keeping crime figures, which required every reported crime to be recorded unless inquiry showed clearly that the report was erroneous or malicious. Before this time, reports of which no confirmation could be obtained, were struck out at the discretion of the local chief officer of police. Consequently there was little uniformity of action. There was, too, a real temptation for the chief officer to cut out doubtful cases which would otherwise swell his station's record of undetected crime.

The result of the present rule may be to include in the statistics some cases where in fact there was no crime, but this is an error on the right side, and over the years these cases probably even themselves out.

The diagram opposite shows the movement of indictable crime in the Metropolitan Police District since 1933.

There was a fairly steady increase until 1941, then a fall in 1942–43, and after that the great increase which brought the total to a record level of 128,954 in 1945. Then for three years the figure slowly fell until 1949–50, when there was a most remarkable fall almost to the figure of 1941. In 1951 the trend was reversed and there was a substantial rise. In 1952 there was a moderate fall, while up to the end of June, 1953, the total was lower than for any corresponding six months since the war and very nearly down to the 1938 total.

As the graph shows, the great majority (ninety-five per cent or over) of indictable crimes are offences against property, either breakings or larcenies, and they are rather more than fifteen per cent higher than in 1938. Larceny can seldom be prevented or detected on the spot, but breakings are very different and it is to these offences that special attention is given. Unfortunately, lack of men made it impossible to give effective cover everywhere, although the wireless car has made up to a remarkable extent for the shortage of men. If a car crew arrives quickly it may forestall the thieves, or at any rate take them red-handed. Even if it fails in this, an early description of them or their car often leads to an arrest when the surrounding area is searched. In either event an immediate arrest saves all the time that an inquiry after the event involves.

A careful analysis is made of the times at which breakings occur and the places are visually recorded in the Map Room, a large room in the basement of Scotland Yard on the walls of which are large-scale maps of the whole Metropolitan Police District. An outcrop of orange flaps on the map of a particular suburb immediately indicates that special attention should be given to this area by the beats and patrols, the wireless cars, and the Flying Squad if necessary. Police dogs, too, have helped in a modest way in dealing with this class of crime, and as the number of dogs increases and their possibilities are more fully realised they will undoubtedly do more.

Although the efforts of the police in dealing with this disturbing form of crime have been less successful than one would have liked, much more has been achieved than might have been

14

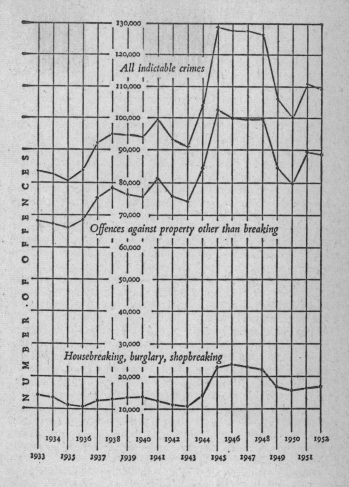

All indictable crimes

Offences against property other than breaking

Housebreaking, burglary, shopbreaking

expected in the circumstances. Since 1949, over twenty-five per cent of the cases reported have been cleared up, compared with nineteen per cent in the years 1933–38. As the force was then practically at full strength, this comparison is highly creditable to the post-war force and shows how the measures taken to improve the transport, communications and public relations of the modern force have to some extent offset the lack of men.

Offences against property involve more police work and more difficult problems than offences against individuals, but they are rarely as sensational and therefore excite less interest, except among the unfortunate victims.

Numerically, offences against individuals, which form a mere fraction of the total crime of the year, amount to only about five and a half per cent of the crimes against property. But since the war they have increased in almost the same proportion. The increase is not in murders, or attempts or threats to murder, or in manslaughter – the figures for these crimes show little change from those of pre-war years – but in woundings and sexual offences.

Wounding is an offence that usually arises from brawls or family quarrels and in most cases the injuries are not serious, but woundings are between thirty per cent and forty per cent higher than they were before the war.

An even more serious rise has taken place in sexual offences. Not only have offences against women increased, but unnatural offences, including indecency between males, are more than three times as numerous as they were before the war. The increase from 224 cases of homosexuality in 1938 to 736 in 1951 is not merely a reflection of greater activity by the police. There can be no doubt that these offences are much more widespread than the figures suggest since, for many years, the police have limited their intervention to cases of open scandal or corruption of boys and young men.

It is a part of the problem that such offences are no longer regarded by a considerable section of the population with the same repugnance as in the past. Our experience in this country is, of course, not exceptional, for a similar if not worse state of affairs is to be found in many other countries, though, either because homosexual practices are not there treated as a criminal offence or because of differences in the law, useful comparison is impossible.

The causes of the increase are hard to assess. It is in line with a general slackening of sexual morals, but more than this is needed to explain the serious increase in perversion.

Inability to face up to the stress of modern life, a reckless pursuit of excitement and pleasure, financial gain, appear again and again in the case-history of offenders. For some, treatment by a psychiatrist may provide a cure, as the experiment started at Wormwood Scrubs before the war has shown. But the proportion of cases susceptible to treatment is clearly limited and the problem seems unlikely to find any quick or easy solution.

It is mainly a West End problem, and involves the police in regular night-time patrols, keeping a lookout for anything suspicious, particularly round public conveniences. This is an unpleasant job that nobody likes, and the patrols, on which young and inexperienced constables are never used, are changed every three months. They patrol in pairs, so that there is always the evidence of two officers, and the Chief Inspector in charge of them is also changed from time to time so that there is no possibility of his becoming too well acquainted with people engaged in this and other forms of vice and exposed to the temptations they can offer.

The activities of the police are mainly directed to preventing the seduction of young men, especially service men who now enter the Forces at eighteen and a half, and there is a close liaison between the Yard and the military authorities in London on this subject.

To offences against individuals should be added robbery with violence, though in the criminal statistics this appears as an offence against property. Since the war there has been a great increase in this form of crime. The peak was reached in 1948, when there were 373 cases, more than three times as many as the average for the five years before the war. After 1948 the number fell steadily and in 1951 was only 214. There was a rise again in 1952 to 298.

Robbery with violence achieves great publicity in the press, and a foreigner reading newspaper reports on the subject might well get the impression that life in London was not unlike that described in the more sensational 'Westerns'. The facts are that in each of the last five years there have been fewer than 300 robberies of this sort in the whole Metropolitan Police District, and in about seventy per cent of these cases no weapon was used, the robber relying on his fists.

So much has been written and spoken on this subject that it is worth while to compare these figures with, for example, those for the United States, published by the Federal Bureau of Investigation. In the first six months of 1953, 'victims of killers', or as we would say murders and manslaughters, numbered 6,470; over 54,000 persons were 'feloniously assaulted by rapists or potential killers', and 29,000 other people were confronted by robbers using guns, other weapons, or force. The population of the United States is about twenty times that of the Metropolitan Police District, but even divided by twenty these figures make our own seem very modest. This is not to belittle the problem, but only to present it in the right proportions.

As I have said, indictable offences include almost all the serious crimes punishable by law, but they represent a relatively small proportion of the offences for which people are prosecuted in court.

Of those arrested by the Metropolitan Police, something like two-thirds are charged with non-indictable offences, while about another 100,000 are summoned at the instance of the police to appear before the magistrates for these, mainly minor, offences. The number of such summonses was greatly swollen during the war and just afterwards by breaches of wartime regulations. The gradual disappearance of these regulations has been very welcome to the police, because it leaves them free to concentrate on really serious crimes. Also, police experience is that a law which does not command general respect is apt to engender a disregard for law in general. In a highly organised society such as ours, some regulations in the general interest are unavoidable, but practical experience makes the police officer agree with those who on other grounds plead that they should be kept to a minimum and only maintained when the necessity is clearly shown. Most police officers would go further and say that unless new regulations can be properly enforced, they had better not be made. From the police point of view a law that cannot be enforced is anathema, whether non-enforcement be the result of a badly conceived or badly worded law, or the creation of so many offences that it is impossible to deal with them all.

Contrary to a very general belief, the urge for additional regulations seldom comes from the police, who in this as in so many matters are more closely attuned to the ideas of the man

18

in the street than many of our legislators, One of the most troublesome and unrewarding tasks of the police, for example, is the enforcement of the law relating to betting and gaming. In no other field, perhaps, is the state of the law so illogical, chaotic and even absurd. It is a patchwork compounded of bits and pieces, some new, some hundreds of years old. It contains in an ill-assorted mixture items reflecting on the one hand the nonconformist's horror of evil and on the other the sportsman's love of an innocent flutter.

Superimposed on this heterogeneous mass of legislation are a series of legal judgements which in the main succeed only in making the confusion worse. Nothing could more plainly call for a thorough clean-up, yet government after government has shied at the prospect and left the task to its successors. Meanwhile the police are expected to carry out the law and not unnaturally, since the law gives them no clear guidance, they have to direct themselves and in effect put their own interpretations upon it. In doing so they have tried to administer the law as far as possible in a common-sense way and to confine their attentions to those forms of gambling which cause public scandal or are clearly operated for gain by clever and unscrupulous people at the expense of more or less innocent victims.

In my evidence before the Royal Commission on Gaming and Lotteries, I suggested that the law ought to be brought into line with practice and that gaming should only be made illegal where it was obviously being carried on as a business for the financial benefit of the promoter. The Royal Commission accepted this view and incorporated it in their recommendations. If it were given legal effect we should escape from the present illogical situation in which an innocent game of poker at the club is illegal, and confine our attention to the much smaller field where there is a real public evil.

At present, action against gaming houses is usually taken under section 6 of the Gaming Act, 1845, which gives the Commissioner of Police power on the application of a Chief Superintendent of Police to issue a warrant authorising the police officers named in it to enter a gaming house, seize any moneys and instruments of gaming, and detain the persons present.

Before such a warrant is applied for, the Superintendent must satisfy himself that gaming is going on, and this can usually be done only by a period of outside observation by police officers, since it is, as a rule, impossible to get into the premises while a game is in progress. When, armed with a warrant, the police have got into the house, the person really responsible is seldom to be found. If the person in charge is convicted, the real owner pays the fine, changes his manager, and after a shorter or longer pause begins again. Some gaming houses have been raided four or five times in a few months, but the profits are evidently large enough to make it worth while to pay the fines and carry on.

But the extent of the evil is often exaggerated. It is mostly confined to lower-class establishments in the West End and East End, and the promoters and players are largely Cypriots, Maltese or coloured people. Occasionally a gaming house in the suburbs becomes notorious and action is taken against it, but such cases are fairly rare.

A much more serious problem is street betting, and here the law is as illogical as it is regarding gaming, with this added disadvantage: that it gives substance to the complaint that there is one law for the rich and another for the poor. Anyone may bet for cash on a racecourse, or place bets on credit with a bookmaker's office. But he may not go to the office to do so or place bets in the street.

There is a tremendous amount of street betting and it takes up a great deal of police time which is only partially effective. The principals are seldom caught, and the fines inflicted on their runners and agents are treated as an expense of the business, so police action can do no more than keep the practice within some sort of bounds.

The serious side of this business is the unhappy fact that from time to time police officers are corrupted. They are few in number and when detected are sternly dealt with, but bookmakers are apt to allege that they have paid 'protection money' to let their runners go free. These allegations are easily made, less easily disproved; time is taken up in investigation; and even if they are untrue – there were no more than two or three proved cases of bribery a year in the whole Force during my Commissionership – they still damage the good name of the police.

It was mainly to meet this problem of street betting that I suggested to the Royal Commission that bookmakers should be registered and cash-betting offices licensed. The system operates satisfactorily in Ireland, and the Royal Commission endorsed the proposal. It would make the work of the police much simpler and would give some prospect of a proper enforcement of the law. No doubt it will be opposed, but such opposition will be hard to justify in view of the fact that the vastly greater amount of gambling on football pools and dog racing remains perfectly legal.

Lotteries cause no great trouble. Police action has been successful in restricting illegal lotteries to a very small scale, and the 1934 Act legalised small private lotteries.

Most police officers take a fairly detached view of gambling. If the country, through Parliament, wishes certain forms to be allowed and others to be banned, they are quite ready to do their best to carry out the intentions of the legislature, but they do ask that the distinction should rest on some recognisably intelligent foundation, and that they should not be saddled with the enforcement of laws which, far from having the backing of public opinion, are regarded by large sections of the population as ridiculous and unjust.

Another unpleasant and difficult task is the enforcement of the law in regard to prostitution and soliciting. Here again the law itself is far from satisfactory, but any attempt to amend it arouses so much controversy that governments are not anxious to burn their fingers in the attempt. The police are frequently criticised for not taking steps for which the law gives them no warrant. Prostitution of itself is not an offence. 'Soliciting to the annoyance of the person importuned' is – but few men, for obvious reasons, are anxious to give evidence in the witness box that they have been annoyed.

Prostitution cannot be stamped out under the existing law, however stringently it is enforced, and every police officer will agree with me that it is doubtful if any conceivable law could have that effect. The police, however, continue to play the role of Mrs Partington, seeking to brush back the Atlantic with her broom. Day after day the melancholy procession of girls and women trails through the courts; they pay fines made inadequate by the fall in the value of money, and return to the beat.

But if the enforcement of the criminal law on this subject is unsatisfactory, the very opposite can be said of the preventive work of the police, and particularly the women police. It is their duty always to be on the look-out for girls and young

21

women in moral danger, and by their wise and sympathetic action they are the means every year of saving many from a life of prostitution and restoring them to their parents or to a decent life.

The administration of the Aliens Order throws a great deal of work on the police, for there are in the Metropolitan Police District about 120,000 registered aliens, chiefly Poles, Russians, Germans and Italians. Between one and two hundred a year are required to leave the United Kingdom under deportation orders made by the Home Secretary, in enforcing which Metropolitan Police officers travel thousands of miles on journeys to all parts of the United Kingdom and many European countries.

It is often suggested that aliens are responsible for the bulk of our crimes, but I am afraid this is wishful thinking. Most of our criminals are home-grown and must be dealt with here. More than once, however, I have put forward the proposal that the law should be amended to enable us to send back to their own countries certain classes of British subjects who are consistent and flagrant law-breakers. Cypriots, Maltese and coloured British subjects are responsible for a disproportionately large part of the offences connected with gaming, living on the immoral earnings of prostitutes, and the sale of drugs and liquor. If they could be sent home on conviction, there would be a distinct improvement in those areas where they are active.

Hitherto the view has been taken that it is of great importance to maintain the principle that any British subject, whatever his race or colour, is entitled to come to the Motherland, or 'home' as so many who have never seen this country affectionately describe it. I can see the political value of maintaining the principle and I would not suggest any general departure from it, but when every other part of the Commonwealth possesses and exercises a power to deport not only aliens but British subjects who offend against the law, it is hard to see why, while maintaining the general right of entry, we should not also have a strictly limited power to remove undesirables who abuse our hospitality. The power need not often be exercised. Its mere existence would be a deterrent, just as the conviction of one of the Messina brothers four years ago had the effect of deterring other members of the family from coming here from Egypt and other Mediterranean countries where they were operating.

Chapter 3
YOUNG MEN IN TROUBLE

AMONG the most ominous of post-war symptoms was the steady rise in crimes committed by young people, and particularly by boys of sixteen and seventeen – the children of the war years. A very few of these were crimes with violence which naturally attracted much public attention.

Many reasons are given for young men taking to crime of this violent kind. I myself am sceptical about the alleged influence of 'thriller' books and films. The normal boy likes excitement as my generation used to enjoy its penny dreadfuls, but I doubt if he often copies deliberately what he reads or sees on the films. He may imitate the externals: the swaggering walk and the boastful methods of the fictional gangster, but this influence does not go deeper than our imitations of Red Indians and pirates.

Many of the boys who get into serious trouble would, I think, have been in trouble anyway, whether they had read books and seen films or not. The common denominator in many of the cases is a broken home. There is nothing stable in the lives of these children, they are early at war with society, and they try to make a world for themselves in substitution for the normal secure life which a child should lead.

Although their home circumstances differed, both Harry Jenkins, who shot Alec d'Antiquis, and Christopher Craig, who shot P.C. Miles at Croydon, had elder brothers already engaged in violent crime. If one member of a family goes wrong, others almost certainly follow, and studies of juvenile delinquency show that the influence of an elder brother is the strongest that can be felt.

The Jenkins family lived in poor circumstances in Bermondsey. In 1945, Thomas Jenkins, elder brother of Harry Jenkins, was among those convicted of the manslaughter of Captain Robert Binney, R.N., who lost his life while trying to intercept a car they were driving over London Bridge after a smash-and-grab raid in the City. The Binney Medal was instituted by some of his friends to be awarded each year to the civilian performing the bravest deed in support of law and order in the Metropolitan Police District or the City of London.

Thomas Jenkins was sentenced to eight years' imprisonment for this affair. Soon after his release he reverted to crime, and in 1953 was concerned in an incident which might well have resulted in a charge of murdering a police officer.

On February 6, 1953, the police received information that thieves intended to rob a wages clerk as he returned to a factory in Chatham Place, Hackney, with money from the bank. To counter this plan they arranged that after the wages clerk left the factory premises for the bank, the manager should keep Chatham Place under observation from a window in the factory and that when the clerk had collected the money he should telephone for further instructions. Meanwhile, if the manager saw anything suspicious he was to telephone Hackney Police Station so that the information could be passed immediately to officers who were watching near the factory.

At about four o'clock that afternoon, the manager saw three men – later identified as Robert Sanders, Thomas Jenkins and John Cracknell – loitering in Chatham Place. He at once telephoned the police station. Shortly before five o'clock, the clerk telephoned for instructions and was told to return to the factory. When his taxi drew up outside, the manager moved to the top of the steps leading to the factory. As the clerk climbed the steps, one of the men followed him. The manager shouted, and the man put his hand into the left breast of his jacket, but the manager lunged at him with an iron bar and he ran away, pursued by the manager and some workmen.

At this moment three police constables, Snitch, Dorsett and Baldwin, who were patrolling in a car, received a wireless message directing them to Chatham Place. When they arrived they saw Jenkins and Sanders running away, and pursued them in the car. At a road junction, however, Sanders and Jenkins separated and the officers continued the chase on foot.

When P.C. Smith was within a few yards of Sanders, he called out that he was a police officer and ordered the running man to stop. Sanders shouted, 'Keep away from me, you bastard, or I'll put a bullet through you!' He then drew a revolver from his pocket and fired. P.C. Snitch dropped to his knees, but got to his feet again as P.C. Dorsett drew level with him. The officers closed with Sanders, who fired two more shots. After a struggle Sanders was disarmed. The revolver was found to contain three spent shells and three live cartridges. P.C. Snitch had a slight wound above the right eye and a bullet-hole through the belt of his raincoat. P.C. Dorsett was unhurt. In the meantime, P.C. Baldwin had caught Jenkins and, after a struggle, arrested him.

Sanders, like Jenkins, was a dangerous and violent criminal, who had escaped a few weeks before from Wakefield Prison, where he was serving a sentence of fourteen years' imprisonment for possessing a firearm with intent to endanger life. The third man, Cracknell, escaped but was arrested later, and on March 30, 1953, at the Central Criminal Court, Sanders was sentenced to imprisonment for life, Jenkins to five years, and Cracknell to three years.

The circumstances surrounding the murder of Alec d'Antiquis on April 29, 1947, were just such a similar fracas in a public street. They also provide an enlightening glimpse into the kind of world in which these things happen.

At about half-past two on that afternoon, there was a hold-up in a pawnbroker's shop in Charlotte Street, Soho. Two men with scarves across their faces attacked the employees with a revolver, firing one or two shots. In the struggle a third man fired a shot from the doorway. Mr Keates, the shop manager, although seventy years old, threw a stool at the two men, who leapt over the counter and ran out to a car, where the third man was waiting. The path of the car was blocked by a lorry, so all three got out and dashed away. As they ran, Mr Keates saw a motor-cyclist turn across their path. Then he heard a shot and saw the motor-cyclist collapse in the gutter. As the men turned into Tottenham Court Road a civilian tripped one of them, causing him to drop the pistol he was carrying; but the man broke away, picked up the pistol and disappeared. The motor-cyclist, Alec d'Antiquis, was given first-aid by a police officer, but died before he got to hospital. He was a motor mechanic with a wife and six young children.

What followed was an excellent example of routine detective work in practice. The three men had been seen by twenty-three people who gave descriptions which, as was perhaps natural among such quickly moving events, did not all tally. Fortunately, Mr Keates was able to give a good description of the two men in the shop and to say which of them had fired at the motor-cyclist.

First, however, the men had to be found. Three days after the crime a taxi driver walked into Tottenham Court Road Police Station and said that at about half-past two p.m. on April 29, he had been driving his cab along the Tottenham Court Road when a man jumped on the running board. The taxi driver brushed him off and saw him run towards the doorway of an office block called Brook House. The police interviewed the office boy there, who said that he had been standing just inside the door when two men pushed him aside and ran upstairs. Later, he saw them leave and noticed that one was no longer wearing the mackintosh he had on when he entered. The first part of the boy's story was corroborated by a lorry driver.

The porter at Brook House had found a car key which the police quickly identified as the key of the car used in the hold-up. The car had been stolen from a street nearby just before the shop was raided. Two days later a painter at Brook House found a man's mackintosh, with a cap and a pair of gloves in the pocket, hidden behind a disused counter. The name-tab on the mackintosh had been removed, but on ripping the coat open, the Chief Inspector in charge of the case found the maker's stock ticket, which showed it had come from Montague Burton Ltd., the multiple tailors. The records of their factory at Leeds showed that the coat had been delivered to one of three branch shops in London. The managers of all three shops were questioned about sales, and the detectives made the long round of innocent purchasers. At last, the manager of the branch at Deptford was able to say from his records that this coat had been sold on November 30, 1946, to a Mr Thomas, of 160 Park Buildings, S.E. 15.

Detectives interviewed Mrs Vera Kemp at this address. She said that the raincoat belonged to her husband, Thomas Kemp, but had been stolen some weeks before at a public house. Kemp himself was intercepted before he reached home and said, after some hesitation, 'that he had lost the coat at the pictures'. Finally he admitted that when he had looked for his coat some time between May 5 and 10, 1947, his wife had said she had lent it to her brother, Charles Henry Jenkins, about a week before.

These inquiries, which had involved interviews with dozens of people, had taken less than a fortnight. On May 11, Jenkins was seen and asked about his movements on April 29. At first he refused to talk, but when the raincoat was shown to him and he was told where it was found he said, 'Except for saying it looks like Tom's coat, I'm not saying any more as it looks serious to me.'

Next day he was seen again, cautioned, and told he would be put up for identification. 'If I get picked out,' he said, 'I'll tell you about the coat, but I shan't tell you where I was until it comes to the last. I'm not having this on my own.'

He was put up for identification on May 13, but none of the witnesses picked him out. He was detained, however, and that afternoon his sister, Mrs Kemp, came to see him.

Jenkins said to her, 'Tell the Chief Inspector who I lent the coat to.'

She replied, with perhaps a little too much readiness, 'Do you mean me to say?'

'Of course,' said Jenkins.

Mrs Kemp then mentioned the name 'Bill Walsh,' and Jenkins added, 'We saw him about a fortnight ago in Southend. He's knocking around with a blonde girl who works in a café on the front. If you like to go to Southend, it would interest you to go to Number thirty-two, I don't know the name of the road.'

The Chief Inspector was interested in this information, not so much for itself as because Jenkins, who was known to the police, was previously noted for his loyalty to associates.

The Chief Inspector went to Southend, but Walsh had left. With the help of the Southend police, however, he did find two watches stolen in an earlier robbery at Queensway, in Bayswater, in which it was suspected that Jenkins had been concerned. The value of the goods stolen had been put at £5,000. A gun used by a twenty-one-year-old man named Geraghty in the same robbery was also discovered, in a shrubbery on the sea front. From one of their informants, the detectives learned that a youth of seventeen named Terence Rolt had been associating with Jenkins. He was brought in and questioned, but though he admitted his association with Jenkins, he professed not to remember where he had been on April 29. Geraghty, too, was brought in and questioned about his movements on that day, but alleged he had been ill in bed. As there was no evidence yet against either Geraghty or Rolt, they were allowed to go.

The detectives then turned their attention again to Jenkins and his sister, Mrs Kemp. According to their statements, Mrs Kemp had lent the coat to her brother and he in turn to Walsh.

27

On May 16, an ex-Metropolitan Police detective-sergeant serving with the Royal Marine Police saw Walsh walking in the street. He had had the man through his hands during his police service, and knew that he was wanted for questioning in the d'Antiquis case. He detained Walsh and handed him over to a Metropolitan Police officer. When Walsh was questioned, he said at once, 'I can see it's serious. I'll tell you about my part in the Queensway job, but I've nothing to do with the Charlotte Street business.'

He then admitted his share in the Queensway robbery with Jenkins, Geraghty and another man, and said that he had gone to Southend and later disposed of the jewellery to various receivers in the East End. He also admitted that on the day before the Queensway robbery, he, Jenkins and Geraghty had reconnoitred the Charlotte Street pawnbroker's premises. On the strength of his statement, Geraghty was detained again. He was cautioned, and in reply said, 'I suppose someone's been chatting since you saw me. You've got them all in, I hear. What I've got to say takes some thinking about.' Later he described in detail the Queensway robbery, which he admitted having carried out with Jenkins, Walsh and another man. In his story, however, he was careful to substitute the name of Walsh for that of Jenkins when speaking of the actual hold-up in the shop. He identified the gun and holster found at Southend and an overcoat found at Jenkins's address as those used and worn by him in the Queensway robbery.

By this time the reason for Jenkins' apparent betrayal of Walsh was obvious. Walsh had slipped away with the whole proceeds of the Queensway robbery, and in retaliation Jenkins had told his story of the loaned raincoat in the hope that Walsh would thereby be implicated in the d'Antiquis murder.

But the story had had repercussions which Jenkins did not intend, for it led first to the questioning of Walsh, then to the implication of Geraghty, whom Jenkins had carefully not mentioned.

All this time the youngest of the men, Terence Rolt, had been kept under observation. On the day after Geraghy's statement he was collected from an address in Bermondsey and taken to Tottenham Court Road Police Station. There he broke down and said unhappily, 'I know it must come out because I see you've got Chris [meaning Geraghty].'

'It's my fault they are here, I bungled it,' he confessed. 'I'll tell you what happened. Chris never meant to kill that man.'

Then he, too, made a statement admitting that he had broken into a warehouse and stolen a number of firearms and a quantity of ammunition which he, Geraghty and Jenkins used in the Charlotte Street hold-up. He described what had happened that afternoon, the shooting, and his escape with Jenkins into Brook House, where Jenkins hid the raincoat and cap.

Jenkins was immediately arrested, and with Geraghty and Rolt was formally charged with murder. Their trial began at the Central Criminal Court before Mr Justice Hallett on July 21, 1947. Geraghty and Rolt admitted the facts, but pleaded that their share did not amount to murder, as the common purpose for which they set out was completed when they robbed the shop.

Jenkins relied on an alibi, but his witnesses were not believed. The trial lasted six days and in his summing-up the judge dealt with the defence of Geraghty and Rolt in the following statement of the law:

'If a private person is trying, in the interests of justice, to stop an escaping felon who is being pursued from the scene of the crime – and the felon must know what is the intention of the private person . . . and the felon nevertheless uses some violent measure to prevent the private person from stopping him, the felon does so at his own risk and is guilty of murder if that violent measure results even unintentionally in the death of the victim.'

The jury, after forty-five minutes, returned a verdict of guilty of murder against all concerned. Geraghty and Jenkins were sentenced to death, and Rolt, being under age, was ordered to be detained during His Majesty's pleasure. Their appeal was unsuccessful, and on September 19, 1947, Jenkins and Geraghty were executed at Pentonville Prison.

There are unfortunately many young men like the two Jenkinses who already in their early twenties seem set in a life of crime. They represent one of the most difficult problems that confronts the penologist. At war with society, they follow

> The ancient rule, the simple plan
> That he shall take who has the power
> And he shall keep who can.

They recognise no law, legal or moral, that stands in their way.
What can and ought we to do about them? 'Treat 'em rough,'

counsel those who believe in the doctrine of repression, and regret the change from the old days of a stern and rigid prison system. Yet rigour alone has never proved effective, and recidivism was as common, or commoner, in the nineteenth century than it is today. How often, in my early days at the Home Office, I found in the records of the habitual criminals of thirty or forty years ago that they had received severe prison sentences in early life which had served only to brutalise them and, by bringing them in contact with older men in prison, to confirm them in a career of crime. Such men came back into the world angry and embittered, and soon took up again with their old companions in crime. It was not long before they returned to prison, and so the sorry circle continued.

Everyone with experience of that old system agrees that it failed. It failed as any system of dealing with human beings must fail that treats them as mere numbers, for however perfect the discipline inside may be, every sentence comes to an end, the prisoner returns to the outside world. The safety-catch is taken off, and unless something more than a compliance with a mechanical discipline has been achieved, he is likely to break out afresh. Indeed, a life in which everything is prescribed and he has no responsibility except to keep out of trouble, will have sapped all initiative and left him even less fitted to meet the stress of life outside than he was when he went in.

For some years now, prison authorities in this and many other countries have sought a new way. It is based on the conviction that every prisoner is an individual, not a number in a register, and that only by using a term of imprisonment, not for punishment, but for training, can we hope to prevent the young offender from developing into the old lag. The Borstal system, by keeping offenders under twenty-one out of prison altogether, has done much, but there still remain the failures of the Borstal system. These are the hard core of the prison problem and to them we in the Prison Commission devoted much thought in the years before the war.

At Chelmsford, we collected a hundred and fifty or so young men round about the age of twenty-five, who had already a number of convictions for serious crime. These young 'specials', as they were called, were then subjected to a regime of strict discipline and vigorous training under an outstanding Governor, Captain Phillips, who had served in the Australian Forces during the first world war. He had his troubles, as I well remember, for they coincided with my assumption of the office of Chairman shortly after. The Dartmoor Mutiny in 1932 had everywhere created a ferment of unrest in our prisons. Captain Phillips combined a firm hand with an understanding heart, and in spite of the unpromising material in his prison his influence was very great; so great, that of his men, somewhere between fifty and sixty per cent. kept out of trouble after release. Such a high proportion was more than we had dared to hope for, and it proved the falsehood of the jibe that 'They all come back'.

On this and similar experiments was founded the new sentence of corrective training for young recidivists. It has not been in operation long enough to judge of its results, but I have no doubt that with a carefully selected staff, the experience of Chelmsford will be repeated. There will inevitably be failures, and they will receive great publicity, but that should not deter us. I do not think we can afford to abandon hope of turning some of these young men back to a decent life, and the gain when we succeed is worth all the cost and effort.

For the failures there remains the new sentence of Preventive Detention, now far more widely used than was possible under the pre-war law. Under it, the hard-bitten recidivist who has failed to respond to other treatments can be put away for a long time for the protection of Society. If his reclamation is rare, at any rate he is prevented for many years from preying on the public.

The two Craig boys were brought up in more comfortable circumstances than the Jenkinses, a reminder that poverty is by no means always the mainspring of crime. Their father was a bank official, and they lived in the residential suburb of Croydon. The elder Craig was first in trouble. At half-past two p.m. on September 14, 1952, information was received by the police that two men named Craig and Burney, who were living at an address in Kensington, were in possession of stolen furs and clothing. Both were said to be armed and likely to use their guns unless they could be taken by surprise. Speed would be necessary, as they intended to dispose of the property quickly.

A detective-inspector and two sergeants, with a police driver, went at once to the address they had been given. The first three went to a room on the second floor, but found the door was locked. Hearing the noise of a window being opened, the

31

inspector ran upstairs and, looking out, saw Burney climbing a stackpipe. He called on him to come down, but instead Burney slid into an open area. The sergeants raced downstairs and found him beginning to climb a ladder into a mews at the back, while the police driver was trying to hold him.

There was a violent struggle. Burney was overpowered and taken back to the room on the second floor, which the inspector had already entered to look for Craig. He was not there, but some stolen furs and clothing were found in a wardrobe. Two officers remained with Burney while the other two went to the next room, the door of which was also locked.

After a while, a woman unlocked the door, and as the police entered, Craig, who had been asleep, woke and reached under his pillow for his gun. The two officers rushed forward and got it away. The safety-catch was off and it was loaded, while in Craig's pockets were a number of rounds of ammunition.

It was afterwards found that both men were wanted for robbery with violence at Waltham Abbey in Essex. They were tried at the Old Bailey and found guilty of robbery while armed and of robbery with violence. Craig was also convicted of possessing a firearm with intent to endanger life, and Burney of receiving. Craig received concurrent sentences of twelve years on each count, and Burney the same on the first two counts and seven years concurrently on the charge of receiving.

The sequel to this sordid crime was an affray such as had not been seen in London since the Battle of Sidney Street in 1910, when Mr Churchill, as Home Secretary, took an active part in the siege of Peter the Painter and his associates.

At quarter-past nine on the night of Sunday, November 2, 1952, a man telephoned Croydon Police Station to say that two men had been seen climbing a gate into a warehouse. About ten minutes later the police arrived in two parties. In a van were Detective-Constable Fairfax, P.C. Harrison, P.C. Pain and P.C. Bugden, and in a wireless car were P.C. Miles and P.C. McDonald. The men were said to be on a flat roof of the warehouse, so Fairfax climbed up a stackpipe and on the roof saw two men near a chimney-stack. He went up to within six feet of them and said, 'I'm a police officer. Come out from behind that stack.'

'If you want us,' said one of the men, who turned out to be Christopher Craig, '– well come and get us.'

'All right,' said Fairfax. He rushed in and grabbed the second man, Bentley, then turned to pursue Craig; but Bentley got away, calling out, 'Let him have it, Chris!'

At once a shot rang out. Shooting is fortunately not common in the streets of London, and Fairfax and his colleagues were unarmed. Fairfax was hit in the shoulder and knocked to the ground. Nevertheless, he got up and tackled Bentley. Another shot was fired, but luckily it missed. Fairfax dragged Bentley behind a rooflight and rapidly searched him, finding a knife and a knuckleduster. He then told Bentley he was going to work him down to a doorway to get cover from the shots, and Bentley warned him that Craig would shoot again.

Soon after this, P.C. McDonald, a heavy man, who had already made an unsuccessful attempt to climb up the stackpipe, called out that he was near the roof but could not manage to get right on to it. Fairfax came out from cover and helped him up the last few feet. He told McDonald he had been hit, and Bentley said, 'I told the silly —— not to use it.'

'Drop your gun,' Fairfax shouted to Craig.

'Come and get it,' Craig answered, and fired another shot which was probably aimed at P.C. Harrison, who had meanwhile climbed up and was creeping along the sloping roof of the warehouse towards the flat roof. He, too, was unarmed. He had his feet in the gutter and his back to the roof, so he was a sitting target for Craig, who fired at him once and probably twice. Harrison, seeing it would be suicide to go on, crept back, climbed down, and came up the staircase with a key to the door leading on to the roof.

It will be noticed that at no point in this battle with an armed and desperate man on a roof-top in the darkness of the night did any policeman think of drawing off and awaiting reinforcements. The police from below, indeed, ran up the stairs, and as they came through the door on to the roof, Craig fired again. The leading policeman, Miles, fell dead with a bullet between his eyes.

Craig came out from behind his chimney-stack and fired once more, this time at the stairs. Harrison, stepping over Miles' body, threw his truncheon at Craig, then a bottle and a block of wood, but missed.

Craig, apparently intoxicated with violence, shouted, 'I am Craig. You've just given my brother twelve years. Come on, you coppers, I'm only sixteen.' As he said this he fired another shot.

'You want to look out,' Bentley said. 'He'll blow your heads off.' Then, as the police began to take him down the stairs, he shouted, 'Look out, Chris, they're taking me down.' Whether or not this was an invitation to fire again, Craig did so.

Meanwhile, news of what was afoot had reached Croydon Police Station, and the station officer on his own initiative – the police had not asked for them – had sent some guns.

The wounded Fairfax, now armed, went back to the roof and shouted to Craig, 'Drop your gun. I also have one.'

He ran towards Craig, firing in the darkness. Craig called out, 'Yes. It's a Colt four-five. Are you hiding behind a shield? Is it bullet-proof? Are we going to have a shooting-match? It's just what I like.'

Then he called to Bentley, 'Have they hurt you, Derek?' After this there were four clicks, a shot, and a cry from Craig, 'There, it's empty.'

As he said this, he took a running dive off the roof and fell almost into the arms of a police officer standing about twenty feet below. Although he was severely injured, he said to those who were holding him, 'I wish I was —— dead. I hope I have killed the —— lot.'

I went down to Croydon early on the morning after this desperate affair and saw Harrison, McDonald and P. C. Jaggs, who had also been on the roof. Fairfax was then in hospital. These three men, who had so worthily upheld the tradition of the Metropolitan Police, were less interested in the night's events than concerned for the widow of the shot policeman, Miles. My impression, indeed, was that I had gone into a family home where one of the family had suddenly died. It is a characteristic of the police that when one of them, or of their families, is in trouble, they give unstintingly whatever help is needed.

Fairfax, whom I saw later, is a pleasant-looking man of medium size; an educated, thoughtful type more like a clerk than a policeman, and a fighting one at that. He minimized his part in the affair, giving me a straightforward account of his actions on the roof, with no attempt at dramatisation. It was part of the day's work. He had done what had to be done.

He made a quick recovery from his wound and was shortly afterwards promoted to sergeant. His gallantry was subsequently recognised by the award of the George Cross. Harrison and McDonald received the George Medal, and Jaggs the

British Empire Medal. The King's Police Medal for Gallantry was awarded posthumously to P.C. Miles. At his funeral service in Croydon Parish Church, a great assembly, which included the Home Secretary and police officers of all ranks, gathered to honour his memory.

Craig and Bentley were in due course committed for trial on a charge of murder. In Bentley's defence, it was urged that though he and Craig had a common purpose when they entered the warehouse, that purpose came to an end when Bentley was arrested, and that he was therefore not guilty of murder. This defence was not accepted, and both he and Craig were convicted. Craig, being under age, was ordered to be detained during Her Majesty's pleasure, while Bentley, having failed in his appeal and the Home Secretary having declined to recommend a reprieve, was executed at Wandsworth Prison.

One reason for the prominence of the two cases I have described was that the murderers used firearms in a public place. They were prominent because in Great Britain this is rare. The number of armed robberies in the Metropolitan Police District each year since the war has varied between ten and forty-six, and although great publicity has been given to this subject in the last year or two, the figures for 1950, 1951 and 1952 – nineteen, ten and nineteen respectively – are in no way abnormal. Relatively small as they are, however, they are too large for comfort, and show the need for strict reinforcement of the Firearms Act, 1937, under which no one may be in possession of a firearm without a certificate from the Commissioner of Police. The arms used by criminals are invariably not covered by a certificate, but have been obtained by theft or other illicit means.

Just after the war large numbers of firearms were being brought to this country by servicemen from overseas theatres of war. Strict measures of control and search in Germany and other places and at the ports of arrival quickly put a stop to this traffic, while an appeal for the surrender of firearms brought in something like 30,000. The conviction of Harry Jenkins and his associates, too, led to the surrender of some guns, and to an immediate, if temporary, drop in violent crime.

Many of the applicants for firearm certificates wish to have a weapon for their personal protection at home, and are apprehensive because of what they have read about attacks on householders. It is only rarely that the burglar or housebreaker carries a weapon, but if it became common for householders to be armed there would be a real danger that the thieves would follow suit and would shoot their way in and out after the manner of a gangster film. This possibility, rather than any fear that the applicant for a firearm certificate is an unsuitable person or has any evil intent, led the Home Secretary to suggest to all Chief Officers of Police shortly after the war a very strict policy in granting certificates.

As Commissioner, I refused a great many applications, especially when the reason given was a desire to protect the applicant in his own dwelling. If that alone were accepted as a reason, there would be no limit to the number of certificates and the position would rapidly deteriorate. The applicant, if dissatisfied with the Commissioner's refusal to grant a certificate, can always appeal to Quarter Sessions. There were few appeals during my Commissionership, and only two were successful.

Cases like those of Jenkins and Craig lead to a suggestion that the police should be armed. The police themselves do not wish it, believing that if they were there would be an increased tendency for the criminal to be armed also and to shoot at sight. In eight years, only two Metropolitan policemen have been shot dead and four or five wounded by firearms – a marked contrast to the United States, where the police are armed and sixty-four were shot dead in the one year – 1951.

We train our policeman in unarmed combat, and that is almost invariably successful in disarming an armed opponent without injury to themselves.

Chapter 4
THE POLICE, THE PRESS, THE PUBLIC

FROM the moment I became Commissioner I was impressed by the keen interest in my job taken by almost everyone I met. I was questioned incessantly about the latest crime, and often my questioner, having read the newspapers, knew more about it than I did. The police touch the life of the ordinary citizen at so many points that this interest is readily understandable. It is reflected in the prominence given to these matters in the press where, more or less truthfully, the doings of the police are chronicled from day to day. The police are 'News' with a capital 'N', and one of my first decisions was that we should be wise to recognise this fact and take advantage of it. In any event, it is impossible to prevent publicity being given to police work even if it were desirable to do so. The newspapers are expert at their job of collecting news, and the days have long gone by when the doings of government departments or the police could be treated as a mystery not to be divulged to the man in the street.

I took every opportunity that was offered to me of lecturing to clubs and organisations of all kinds on the work of the police, and a story I often used to tell was that of the old police sergeant who, when the first telephone was introduced at Scotland Yard, shook his head sadly and remarked, 'I don't know what we're coming to. At this rate it won't be long before the public starts ringing us up.'

This attitude of mind remained to some extent when I reached Scotland Yard, and I well remember the horror of one of my senior officers when I announced that I had agreed to allow a press photographer to take a picture of one of my morning conferences. I had to dissuade him from hiding his face behind a sheet of paper when the photograph was taken.

I firmly believed, however, that the public, which pays something over eighteen million pounds a year for the Metropolitan Police, is entitled to know what is being done by the Force and what value it is getting for its money. One of my first acts

37

was to get approval for the appointment of a Public Information Officer. There was already a small press bureau at Scotland Yard which gave out a limited amount of information on police matters, but its members had no experience as journalists and I felt it was essential, if our relations with the press were to be put on a satisfactory basis, that the officer in charge of the bureau should be someone who knew the ways and the people of Fleet Street.

I was fortunate in obtaining the services of P. H. Fearnley who, after many years in the newspaper world, had also had experience as press officer in the B.B.C., the War Office and in India. His title was carefully chosen as Public *Information* Officer, to emphasise that the object of the new appointment was the distribution of information, and to avoid the criticism, so often levelled at Public Relations Officers, that they exist only to praise or excuse their ministers or departments.

Soon afterwards, I invited the news editors of the London dailies to meet me, and after giving them a frank review of the crime situation, which at that time was causing great anxiety, I told them that my policy would be to give the fullest and earliest information to the press on police activities, subject only to the necessity to avoid publication of information which might interfere with an inquiry in progress or with the course of justice. That policy has been followed ever since, with results which have been satisfactory to both sides.

Confidences have almost invariably been respected, and the public has had the benefit of authentic news. Not always, however. Once, during investigations into a murder case, I was on holiday in Devon when the waiter told me that, according to his morning paper, I had held a midnight conference at Scotland Yard with Ronald Howe, my Assistant Commissioner, Criminal Investigation Department. Still more surprising was the news, which I read in a Dutch paper, at Scheveningen one Monday morning, that I had broken my stay in Holland and flown to London the Saturday before, to hold another midnight conference.

When I taxed the reporter responsible for this, he said blandly, 'Oh, well, it makes a good story.' I should have thought it indicated something wrong with an organisation when midnight conferences had to be held so often; but perhaps, in Fleet Street, they have to be. These little errors did not affect my belief in the value of good relations with the press or my endeavours to maintain them. They have certainly been of the greatest value to the police. The case which I have often quoted as the classic example of co-operation between the three P's – police, press and public – was the arrest of the murderer of P.C. Nathaniel Edgar.

Edgar, a man of thirty-three, joined the Metropolitan Police in 1939, and after three years' service in the Royal Navy during the war he returned to police duty in 1946. He was married and had two small boys. In the winter of 1947-48 there was an outbreak of housebreaking in the Highgate and Southgate areas, and to combat it a number of uniformed officers were attached as aids to the Criminal Investigation Department. They worked in plain clothes and were moved from one part of the Division to another as they were needed.

One of these officers was Edgar. On the afternoon of February 13, 1948, he was patrolling in the Southgate area with P.C. McPartlan. At about eight in the evening, the two officers parted in the hope of locating a suspect whom they had been following earlier on. Not long after, a Mrs Laing telephoned the Information Room at Scotland Yard and reported that while she was out walking with her brother she had heard three shots and almost at once had seen a man run along Broadfields Avenue from Wades Hill and disappear. She and her brother turned into Wades Hill, and in the garage entrance of Number 112 saw Edgar lying on the ground, groaning and bleeding profusely.

Police officers in a wireless car went at once to Wades Hill, and Edgar was able to tell them, 'The man was by the door. I got his identity card and name. He shot me in the legs with three shots. The pocket-book is in my inside pocket.' In the pocket-book was the following entry: 'M or (Mr) Thomas Donald, 247 Cambridge Road, Enfield, BEAH 257/2.' Then Edgar became unconscious. He died in hospital at half-past nine that night from three bullet wounds in the right groin and right thigh.

Edgar was the first policeman shot on duty for very many years, and the case naturally made a deep impression on his fellows. The police have no particular animus against criminals. Indeed, they develop a great understanding of human nature under stress and learn to make allowances for it. But they would be more than human if the murder of a colleague did not put them immediately on their mettle. I was telephoned at my home that night with news of Edgar's death and the grim assurance that the murderer would be found.

The Divisional Detective Inspector had no difficulty in identifying the 'Thomas' of Edgar's notebook as Donald George Thomas, a deserter wanted since October 13, 1947, but he was not to be found at his home in Enfield. I saw Howe at Scotland Yard early next morning, and for the first time we issued to the press that form of words which has since become well known, stating that the police urgently wished to interview Donald George Thomas, who was believed to be able to help them in their inquiries. This was seen by a Mr Stanley J. Winkless of Camberwell, who reported that Thomas had visited his home occasionally. Mrs Winkless, his wife, had been missing for three weeks, and he thought she was in Thomas's company. He gave the police a photograph of his wife, which we decided to issue to the press.

There were immediate results. Reproductions of the photograph appeared in the morning editions on February 17. At half-past seven that morning a Mrs Smeed, who kept a boarding house in Clapham, saw the photograph and showed it to her husband, saying she thought it was that of a woman who was then sharing their top front room with a man. Mr Smeed found a police officer and told him of their suspicions. The officer at once telephoned the Information Room at the Yard and kept watch on the house. In a few moments a wireless car arrived with three officers, and soon afterwards Inspector Moody came from Brixton Police Station. He arranged that Mrs Smeed would take up breakfast as usual to the top front bedroom, and with the other officers he followed her upstairs.

Mrs Smeed laid the tray on the floor, knocked at the door, heard a voice from inside say, 'Okay,' then went downstairs. The officers waited tensely outside the door until they heard the key turn in the lock. The door opened, and Thomas, dressed in vest and pants, looked through the crack. Seeing the officers, he slammed the door at once, but they burst into the room, and as they did so Thomas made a leap for the bed and put his hand under the pillow.

The three officers flung themselves upon him and the inspector seized his right hand, in which was a gun. There was a short, violent struggle, the gun was taken from him, and he was held.

The inspector cautioned Thomas and asked, 'Is the gun loaded?'

'That gun's full up,' Thomas replied, 'and they were all for you.'

As he was being taken to the police station he said, 'You were lucky. I might just as well be hung for a sheep as a lamb.'

In his room the police afterwards found seventeen rounds of point three-five ammunition, a rubber truncheon, a jemmy, a number of identity cards and an instruction book called *Shooting to Live with the One-Hand Gun*. Published in 1942, it was written by two Commandos, Captain W. E. Fairbairn and Captain E. A. Sykes, and described, according to the preface, 'methods developed and practised during an eventful quarter of a century and adopted, in spite of their unorthodoxy, by one police organisation after another in the Far East and elsewhere. It is the authors' hope that their relation of these methods may contribute to the efficiency, and therefore safety, of those whose lot it is to use the one-hand gun in the course of duty.' Some chapter headings of the book are: 'Purposes of the pistol', 'Choosing a pistol', 'Training: Preliminary course for recruits', and 'Training: Advanced methods'.

Thomas's Lüger automatic, when it was examined at the police station, contained eight rounds in the magazine and one in the breech. Mrs Winkless later told the police that Thomas had confessed to her that he had shot Edgar. Thomas himself refused to say anything, except to give a false account of his movements on the night of the shooting. Examination of the bullets found in Edgar's body established clearly that they had been fired from Thomas's gun.

Thomas's background was revealing. He was born on July 16, 1925, and at the school in Edmonton, which he left at fourteen, he was classed intellectually among the best half-dozen boys. He was captain of the cricket eleven and a member of the Boys' Brigade. He began work as a telegraph messenger, became a junior clerk, and was in trouble with the police before his sixteenth birthday. Twelve months' probation was followed by further offences, but a spell at an approved school during the war seems to have been effective, for when he came out he began to study mathematics and electrical engineering at a technical school. He was called up for military service in January, 1945, however, and deserted a fortnight later. After two years on the run, he surrendered to the military police, served 160 days' detention, and almost immediately after his release deserted again. He had been absent some three months when he shot Edgar.

At his trial, Thomas was found guilty of murder. At the time, however, the death penalty was in suspense as a result of a vote in the House of Commons against capital punishment, and the death sentence on Thomas was accordingly commuted to penal servitude for life – a decision which was not unnaturally viewed with critical feelings by police officers. It is also one likely to present some future Home Secretary with an awkward problem if and when the question of Thomas's possible release comes to be considered.

I could quote many other cases in which press and public have aided the police. John Edward Allen, a child-murderer, who escaped from Broadmoor, remained at liberty for two years until his photograph, published in an evening newspaper, came to the notice of the proprietor of the bakery in which he was employed under the name of Kenneth Watts. On another occasion the Glasgow police needed urgently the photograph of a wanted man. There was no time to send it by post or train, but by courtesy of one of the London daily papers the photograph was telegraphed to Glasgow within an hour or two and enabled the police there to clinch their identification.

The complaint is often made, however, that the press give too much prominence to the details of violent crimes, and by doing so provide the criminal, and especially the adolescent criminal, with a notoriety which he enjoys. There is substance in this view, and I would like to see these matters dealt with in a far less sensational way; for, apart from the effect on the individual offender, it is an axiom among experienced police officers that if great publicity is given to a sensational crime it will almost certainly be followed by others of a similar kind.

There is unfortunately no question that crime, and violent crime in particular, is greatly above the pre-war level, and no one, least of all the police, would wish this disturbing state of affairs to be regarded with indifference or complacency. Only if the seriousness of the situation is widely realised will it be possible to secure public support for strengthening the forces of law and order. But in drawing attention to this situation it is easy to create a false impression. Every year there are good and bad periods. In the long winter evenings the crime figures always go up, for the obvious reason that, under cover of the dark, the criminal can pursue his trade with far less risk of detection. The four days of exceptionally dense fog in December, 1952, brought an epidemic of bag snatching, assaults and burglaries, which doubled our normal figures for the week.

If such a series of incidents is announced by the press as a crime wave and publicity is given to every case, the public become so alarmed that old people barricade themselves in their houses at night and others believe it is unsafe to go out after dark. Yet frequently the rise turns out to be only temporary and after a a week or two crime falls off and the publicity campaign dies away. It is an odd thing, too, how frequently public alarm at a particular form of crime reaches its peak when the indications are that the occasion for alarm is passing. So far as the Metropolitan Police District is concerned, the lastest example is the agitation which led to the passing of the Prevention of Crime Act, 1953, dealing with offensive weapons.

In 1947 and 1948, robbery with violence was more than three times as frequent as in pre-war years, and there was a corresponding increase in the use of firearms by robbers. But since 1948, robberies have decreased from 373 to 298 in 1952, and there have been far fewer cases in which firearms, a cosh or other weapons have been used.

On this occasion, too, there was a body of opinion led by some of H.M. judges which regarded the abolition of corporal punishment in the Criminal Justice Act, 1948, as a grave error and quoted the reports of sensational crimes as a confirmation of their view, notwithstanding that crimes formerly punishable by flogging have continued to decrease since its abolition. The result of this dual agitation was the passing of the Prevention of Crime Act, 1953, under which it was made an offence for anyone who could not show lawful authority or reasonable excuse, to have on him in any public place an offensive weapon; and a police officer was given power to arrest him without warrant if not satisfied of his identity or place of residence, or if he had reasonable cause to believe that it was necessary to arrest him to prevent him committing any other offence in which he might use an offensive weapon. It is too early to say what has been the effect of the new law, for so far there have been very few occasions when it has been used.

At the time of one agitation, when a general alarm was aroused by the publicity given to a series of violent crimes, I took the unusual course of announcing that in two or three cases there had proved on inquiry to be no crime at all. In one instance a girl had given a lurid account of having been assaulted; this she had done in order to explain to her parents why she had stayed out so late at night. In another case a careless watchman invented a story of a nocturnal attack to cover the results of his negligence. Rather to my surprise, this unconventional move was welcomed by the press, and the crime wave subsided both in print and in fact.

It is easy to criticise the press and to forget the pressure under which the modern newspaper is produced, and if I have referred to some things which might perhaps be better arranged, I do so in no spirit of captious criticism. I should be ungrateful if I did, for it was only with the help of the press that I was able to let the public know something of our problems and to gain from them during the difficult post-war years a sympathetic understanding of the special problems created by our lack of men.

Publicity became, in fact, an indispensable part of our armoury, and we did not limit our activities to the daily press. We gave assistance to the writers of articles in periodicals of all kinds and co-operated in the production of numerous programmes on wireless and television. Perhaps the most successful in warning the public how to help themselves was a series on the wireless entitled, 'It's Your Money They're After', in which various types of fraud were described and hearers were warned to be on their guard. The cinema, too, offered great opportunities. Besides giving facilities for many documentary films on the work of various departments, we co-operated with Ealing Studios in making *The Blue Lamp*, which gave a faithful picture of the policeman's life and work in the form of an exciting crime story, much of the detail of which was taken from actual happenings in recent crimes. This film has been shown all over the world and has been a valuable means of spreading a knowledge of the efficiency and high traditions of the Metropolitan Police.

In addition to these methods of publicity, we have organised frequent exhibitions at Olympia, in the big departmental stores and in halls and cinemas, illustrating the work of the police and conveying, by way of pictures and models, advice to the public on ways in which they can protect their homes by such simple measures as fastening their windows at night and fitting efficient door-locks. These methods have no doubt had good results, but it is a never-ending battle to combat the thought-lessness and carelessness which are so often the allies of the criminal.

Something like half the entries into houses and flats are made by way of doors and windows which have been left open or unfastened, and, in spite of repeated warnings, householders still continue to advertise their absence when they go away by leaving newspapers and milk bottles to accumulate on the doorstep or by putting notices on the door saying, 'Away until Monday'. The limit of carelessness was reached by the lady who left her pearls overnight in a car in the courtyard of a block of flats in the West End. When, inevitably, they were stolen, she came to us, and by great good fortune we were able to recover them from a receiver in the East End. One would have thought experience would have brought wisdom, but no: the lady left them in her car again a few nights later, and when the report came in that they had been stolen a second time, I must admit that my comment was, 'Serve her right!'

It is not only the householder who offers opportunities to the thief. Many business firms invite theft by the way they send their takings or fetch their wages from the bank. Clever thieves conduct their reconnaissance with the same care and attention to detail as a military officer, and a messenger who always takes the same route at the same hour is easy meat. It is one of the recognised tasks of the Criminal Investigation Department to remind firms of these and other risks that should be obvious, and to advise them on the steps they should take to safeguard their property.

Many films have installed various types of burglar alarm in their factories and business premises. Some of them are so arranged that when a window or door is opened an automatic device operates the telephone and dials 999. This calls the Information Room at Scotland Yard and a gramophone record recites the address and the fact that burglars have entered the building. This information is at once sent by radio to a patrolling police car, and often the police arrive in time to find the thieves still on the premises. On one night, an alarm in a single factory was set off three times by three different parties of burglars, and three sets of very astonished criminals were duly brought in to await their fate.

It is the telephone, so dreaded by the elderly police sergeant, which has been the biggest single factor in helping the public to assist a depleted police force in their struggle against crime. In July, 1937, an arrangement was made with the G.P.O. whereby, if a London caller dialled 999, he could be put on at once to the police, the fire or the ambulance service. The service has since been steadily extended all over the country. The number of such calls to the Metropolitan Police has grown steadily from about 35,000 in 1945, to 110,000 in 1952. In the same period the number of arrests by the crews of wireless area cars has gone up from 4,462 to 11,000. Of course, a good many calls are made too late or by mistake, but it is well worth while to suffer these abortive calls when something like one in ten results in an arrest. Not only does an arrest put a stop to the operations of a thief who, if undetected, might go happily on night after night until finally caught with a total of fifty or more cases to his credit (or debit); but when a thief is caught red-handed, there is an enormous saving in the valuable time of detective officers who would otherwise have to start on their investigations from scratch.

I seized every opportunity of publicising the 999 system and encouraging the public to make use of it. The response was remarkable and information came in from most unlikely quarters. One case that especially pleased me concerned two small boys about eight years old, who used to play in the street near the gateway to a busy goods yard in the East End of London. The drivers of the heavy lorries entering the yard got to know the boys, and as they drove by, greeted them with a cheery word and a smile. One day a lorry drove out, but instead of the usual greeting the boys received only a scowl and a curse.

'That's funny,' said the elder. 'There's something wrong here. You get his number and I'll dial 999.' As a result of their action the lorry was stopped by a police car and was found to be loaded with stolen goods. The story had a happy ending – for the boys – when a few days later a police inspector visited their school and in the presence of their schoolmates thanked them on my behalf and gave them a small gift in recognition of their smart work.

The centre of the Metropolitan Police communication system is the Information Room in the basement at Scotland Yard. This focal point is connected by a private telephone system with all police stations, police boxes and telephone pillars. There are 400 blue police boxes and telephone pillars all over

London, each connected by direct line to its local station, and through them the officer on the beat can report any matter that needs attention or can be called by the flashing light at the top of the box. The Information Room is also the centre of a teleprinter network which extends to every District, Divisional and Sub-divisional station and District garage. Through this network, instructions can be broadcast simultaneously over as wide an area as necessary, and it has the great advantage of providing a typewritten record of all messages.

The Information Room's trump card in speed of communication, however, is its direct two-way wireless telephony link with 117 wireless area cars, each manned by two or more constables who patrol every division throughout the twenty-four hours; with forty-eight Traffic and Accident Group cars and motor-cycles; with the river launches of the Thames Division; and, certainly not least, with the 'Q' cars, not easily recognisable as police cars, and other vehicles of the Criminal Investigation Department's Flying Squad.

The Information Room is staffed day and night by officers with long experience of police work, and to them comes a steady stream of messages from police stations, police on the beat or in cars, motor-cycles and river craft, and from members of the public dialling 999. On four glass-topped tables in the Information Room are large-scale maps of the Metropolitan Police District, on which counters of varying shapes and colours represent all the vehicles and boats in commission. When one of them is called up and sent on a duty, or is for any reason out of action, a coloured ring is placed round it so that the officers in the Information Room can see at a glance what units are available and which are nearest to the place where police are wanted. Similarly, the Traffic and Accident Groups can be diverted to places where accidents or hold-ups call for attention, and since 1951 a number of motor-cycles have also been subject to wireless call from the Information Room.

When great crowds or heavy traffic are expected, as, for instance, at the Derby or the Coronation, some or all of the ten communication vans are brought into use and through them the officers in charge are able to obtain from the control room, which is set up specially for the occasion, a full picture of conditions beyond their own area and can summon help if the situation seems liable to get out of hand.

Walkie-talkie radio has also been used with good results to supplement the communication vans and traffic patrols on busy days, or to summon reserves when disorder has been threatened. Similarly, the C.I.D., when watching premises where they expect a crime to be committed, sometimes arrange for one officer with walkie-talkie equipment to keep observation and summon the main party to the scene only when the time is ripe for their appearance.

In April, 1953, there was a collision between two Underground trains in the tunnel between Stratford and Leyton Stations. Ten people were killed and fifty seriously injured. Through the Information Room at Scotland Yard, Fire and Ambulance Services from London, Essex and West Ham were summoned, and the police from 'K' Division were early on duty, conveying nurses, doctors and equipment to the scene. A walkie-talkie service was set up by police and although, owing to the amount of metal in the tunnel, messages could only be sent comparatively short distances, a satisfactory service was maintained all through the night until the line was cleared at ten o'clock the next morning.

I never failed to be fascinated by the Information Room at work. At one end of the long, green and white room is the switchboard to which all Scotland Yard 999 calls come. At the other is the microphone through which a constant stream of messages is passed from 'M2GW,' the Information Room's call-sign, to the divisional cars and boats.

Information Room and the wireless cars between them have some smart captures to their credit. On one afternoon in March, 1950, for instance, an emergency message was received from Speedwell Telephone Exchange reporting that a call for police had been received from an address at Golders Green. A wireless car and a 'Q' car were directed to the spot. The crew of the wireless car, who were first on the scene, found that three men had forced their way into the house, bound and gagged a maid, and after stealing some property had made their getaway. Descriptions of the men were obtained and the district searched. Within twenty minutes two of the wanted men had been arrested, and after a prolonged search by the crew of the 'Q car, the third man was also found. On another occasion a message was received from the watchman of a Stratford factory, reporting the suspicious conduct of the driver of a car which was stationary outside. A wireless car arrived, to find the car unattended. As the revenue licence on the car appeared to have been altered, the officers sent the engine and chassis numbers to Information Room by radio-telephony for a check to be made. Within a few minutes Information Room told the crew that the car was stolen and the index plates were false. The crew watched until the driver returned, and he admitted having stolen the car from Picca-dilly.

And of course there are the unfailingly exciting car chases, generally at night, along the deserted London streets. Perhaps the most famous of these followed a report from the Surrey police that thieves had broken into a golf club near London and stolen a large quantity of whisky. A warning was at once wirelessed to all police cars in south-west London, and within a few minutes the crew of a wireless car reported that they had seen a black saloon which seemed to answer the description given, and were following it northwards along the main road from Staines to London. When this message came in, two other wireless cars were ordered to try and intercept the black saloon. Meanwhile the thieves, realising that they were being followed, put on speed. When they found it impossible to shake off the police car, they began bombarding it with bottles of whisky, intending to smash the windscreen. But they missed, and when the intercepting police cars appeared ahead of them they swerved to avoid them and crashed into a telegraph post, so ending an exciting chase.

As an indication of the volume of work the Information Room has to deal with, during June, 1953, 12,030 calls came in from police stations, 1,426 from police officers, and no fewer than 10,389 from members of the public; a significant indica-tion of the way in which swift communications, a mechanised police and an alert public have enabled a depleted police force to keep its end up during these post-war years, when crime has increased so alarmingly and the criminal has turned to his own uses modern means of rapid movement.

This system of communications extends overseas, through the International Criminal Police Commission, a body on which the police of nearly fifty countries are represented by their Chief Officer or by senior officers of their criminal investi-gation departments. The Commission has a wireless network radiating from Paris and covering all European countries out-side the Iron Curtain, over which requests and information can be sent with great speed. The Secretariat regularly circulates information about international criminals, as a result of which frequent arrests have been made. A special part of the Commission's work is the branch office in Holland dealing with forgery and counterfeiting at which, with the help of national central offices of police, a very complete collection of every kind of forged or counterfeited currency is maintained. By this means a constant check is kept on the activities of the gangs responsible for making and circulating forged notes, and the police of the various countries concerned are able to co-operate in fighting this illegal traffic.

In this country, Scotland Yard acts as the national central office, on behalf of all police forces, and the Information Room is in constant wireless communication with Paris. The number of messages exchanged has increased steadily each year since the war, and in 1952 numbered something like two thousand.

Striking evidence of public co-operation with the police is to be found in the records of the Selection Committee which every year awards the Binney Medal. Each year police reports of brave acts by civilians in support of law and order are submitted to a committee consisting of the Commissioners of Police for the City and the Metropolis, the Chief Magistrate, the Fourth Sea Lord and the Clerk of the Goldsmiths Company, who are Trustees of the Fund. The number of cases submitted to the Committee has risen steadily, and the Committee were so impressed by the standard of courage revealed by these stories that a few years ago, on the proposal of Lord Mountbatten, who was then a member, they decided to give certificates to men and women whose conduct, while not quite achieving the medal, revealed the requisite standard of bravery. So far, thirty certificates have been awarded, of which six have gone to women.

The Binney Medal for 1950 was awarded to Mr Thomas Temple of Biggin Hill. On the night of September 27, Mr Temple was wakened shortly before one o'clock by a private burglar alarm operating from the shop next door, of which he was the manager. He called the local police and some other persons connected with the shop, dressed, and went out into the street. At that moment the police arrived, and after a quick examination of the premises, Mr Temple and one of the constables went in, leaving the others to cover the shop from outside. As Mr Temple and the constable approached the office on the first floor, a man stepped out, raised a revolver and fired in their direction. Immediately afterwards he was joined by another man and they both ran from the office and disappeared round a corner. Mr Temple and the policeman, undeterred by the revolver shot, followed. As the policeman started to grapple with the second man, the first turned and fired two more shots, one of which hit the constable in the neck. Then the two men ran downstairs, still pursued by Mr Temple.

The men separated, and soon a crash of glass told Mr Temple that one, at least, was being dealt with by the police outside. He returned to help the officer who had been shot, and found him lying on the floor with the second man on top of him. Mr Temple picked up a wooden batten, drove the policeman's assailant off, and held him in a corner until help arrived.

I met the winner of the 1951 Binney Medal, Mrs Phyllis Holman Richards, several times. She was a slight, middle-aged lady of medium height and by no means fighting build. On the morning of April 17, two men armed with heavy metal bars attempted a smash-and-grab raid on a jeweller's shop in Sloane Street. One broke the shop window while the other stood guard on the pavement. A third man waited close by in a stolen motor car. A police officer in plain clothes happened to be near, and he at once tackled the man at the shop window. The man on the pavement went to help his companion and together they began to attack the policeman with their metal bars.

At this moment Mrs Richards was getting off a bus a short distance away. Calling for help, she ran to the second man and grasped his arm to prevent him from striking the officer again. Although she was in great danger of serious injury herself, she held on to him until further help arrived. Both men were eventually arrested, and when they appeared in court the magistrate complimented Mrs Richards on her courage. Her own comment to me was that far too much had been made of the affair, she had just run over when she saw what was happening. Against such women, criminals may well feel that they fight in vain.

They in turn are served by a police force second to none. Every year during my Commissionership there came to Scotland Yard visitors from police forces all over the world to see and study the methods of the Metropolitan Police. Some came with the definite purpose of inquiring into what they regarded as the mystery of the good relations between the Metropolitan Police and the London public. In their own countries the police were often looked at as a race apart, if not, indeed, as the enemy of the man in the street.

'How is it,' they would ask, 'that in London the policeman is regarded by every law-abiding citizen as a friend and helper?'

My reply was always that this relationship is not to be achieved in a day, and that it is necessary to begin a hundred years ago, with the sound principles laid down by Mayne and Rowan. Successive generations of police recruits have been schooled to regard themselves not as masters but as servants of the public. They have been taught that even when presenting a case against an offender they must be scrupulously fair, and that having put the case before the court, their duty is done and they are not concerned with the verdict. If there is anything to be said in favour of the accused, it must not be withheld from the court after conviction, and if a piece of evidence favourable to the accused comes to light during their inquiry, it must as a matter of course be communicated to the defence.

As an illustration of the care taken to avoid any unfairness, the following case is by no means unique. A few months after the introduction of the no-waiting restrictions in London, under which it was an offence to park a car in any street marked by a yellow band on the lamp-posts or in the first fifteen yards of a side-street leading into a yellow-band street, it was discovered that the marking in the side-streets had by an error been placed too far from the main road by several yards. A number of motorists had already been summoned, and some had been convicted, for parking their cars in the marked areas, though, in fact, their cars might have been further back than the distance prescribed by the regulations. At once instructions were issued that the file relating to every case should be examined. Where a prosecution was pending it was withdrawn, and where there had already been a conviction, a recommendation was made to the Home Secretary, and acted upon, that a Free Pardon should be granted.

'A beast, but a just beast' – the schoolboy's opinion of his headmaster – would probably in most cases be the law-breaker's verdict on the police. Many a prisoner, after his sentence has been served, has had reason to be grateful to the police officers who brought him to justice, for they also helped him to get back into employment.

In Ireland before the Treaty, and recently in Malaya, we have seen the difficulties of a police force surrounded by a hostile or an intimidated population. Without public backing no force can hope to do its work successfully. It takes a long time to gain such confidence, but it could be lost very quickly as a result of stupid or overbearing conduct on the part of a few officers. No one realises this better than the police themselves, and they are the first to condemn conduct which might let the side down. As a result they can invariably count on the help of the public in maintaining the Queen's Peace.

Chapter 5
THE HAIGH CASE

In one outstanding case during my Commissionership, the press caused Scotland Yard so much anxiety that at one stage it seemed likely that we might have to abandon our main charge against John George Haigh.

The murder of Mrs Durand-Deacon by Haigh is among the most gruesome that Scotland Yard has had to deal with. One of the most surprising features of the case was the contrast between Haigh's elaborate method of destroying the body and his absurd over-confidence. He made no real attempt to conceal his movements or the proceeds of his crime. It is often said that a criminal forgets some little thing which gives him away, but here there was no question of forgetting. Encouraged by past successes, apparently believing that where there is no body there can be no murder charge, Haigh contemptuously left a trail of clues that could not fail to be picked up once inquiries began. Moreover, he took it upon himself to ensure that inquiries did begin. At about two o'clock on the afternoon of February 18, 1949, Mrs Durand-Deacon, a lady of sixty who had lived for some time at the Onslow Court Hotel, South Kensington, told her friend, Mrs Lane, that she was going to meet Mr Haigh.

'We're going down to his place,' she said, 'where he experiments on different things.'

She was never seen again.

On the day after her disappearance, Haigh himself went to Mrs Lane at the hotel and asked if Mrs Durand-Deacon was ill.

'I was to have picked her up at the Army and Navy Stores,' he said. 'I waited for her until five-and-twenty to four, then I went away.'

The next day he inquired about her again, and when Mrs Lane said that she intended to report the matter to the police, Haigh said he thought they had better go together. They accordingly went to Chelsea Police Station, where Haigh especially asked that his name should be taken.

On February 21, Woman Police Sergeant Lambourne was put on to make routine inquiries about a missing woman, one of many who are reported to the police every week. There was as this stage nothing to distinguish Mrs Durand-Deacon's disappearance from any other. Sergeant Lambourne, however, saw Haigh, and with that seventh sense which the good policeman – or -woman – acquires, reported to her superiors that she suspected something wrong.

Haigh, having drawn attention to himself, now could not escape the searchlight. He was interviewed that same day by the Divisional Detective Inspector, and said that he was a director of Hurstlea Products Ltd, a firm with a factory at Crawley, where he usually went once or twice a week. He had known Mrs Durand-Deacon for three years. Following a discussion with her about an idea she had for a new type of artificial finger-nail, he had suggested that it might be possible to do something about manufacturing such nails, and he had arranged to take her to Crawley on the afternoon of February 18. They were to meet at half-past two p.m. at the Army and Navy Stores. Just before that time he saw her leave the hotel, dressed in a black hat and a black astrakhan coat, with a brass crucifix on a chain round her neck, and carrying a red plastic handbag.

According to Haigh, Mrs Durand-Deacon failed to keep the appointment at the Stores, and after he had waited nearly an hour, he went to Crawley alone. He then gave an account, afterwards found to be untrue, of his movements at Crawley that afternoon.

Haigh was questioned several times and on February 26, at the request of the Chelsea Police, a detective-sergeant of the West Sussex Constabulary went to a storehouse in a builder's yard at Leopold Road, Crawley, which belonged to Hurstlea Products Ltd. There he found three carboys containing what seemed to be acid, a leather attaché case, and a large leather hat-box marked H. In that hat-box was a point thirty-eight six-chambered Enfield revolver with eight rounds of ammunition, papers in the names of Mrs Rosalie Mary Henderson, Dr Archibald Henderson, Donald McSwan, William Donald McSwan and Amy B. S. McSwan. In the attaché case were more papers bearing the names of the McSwans, and a contract note in Haigh's name. In a ration book there was a receipt dated February 19 from the Cottage Cleaners, Reigate, for a Persian lamb coat.

When Haigh was interrogated about this receipt later in the day, he said it was for a coat belonging to Mrs Henderson. The staff at the cleaners, however, remembered the coat having been handed in by a man on February 19, and after it had been inspected by Mrs Durand-Deacon's sister, her friend Mrs Lane, and the manageress of the hotel, little doubt was left that the coat was the one Mrs Durand-Deacon had been wearing on the day she disappeared. Its identification was put beyond doubt when some pieces of material found in Mrs Durand-Deacon's room were examined in the Laboratory at Scotland Yard. There it was found that the raw edges of one piece of material exactly fitted the raw edges of the material left in the sleeve of the coat when a repair had been made, and that another piece showed areas of wear corresponding exactly to those on a strip of the same material which had been used to mend the bottom of the coat.

As a result of articles in the press about the disappearance of Mrs Durand-Deacon, a pawnbroker at Horsham came forward with information about some jewellery which a man had brought in on February 19. As the owner of the shop was out, the man had left the jewellery and called again on the 21st. The articles were valued at £131, and consisted of five rings, a paste necklet and clip, a pair of ear-rings, an opal tie-pin in a red case, a double row of cultured pearls, and an emerald and diamond snap. Though the man gave a different name the assistant had recognised him as J. G. Haigh of Onslow Court Hotel, with whom he had done some business in 1948.

The next day – when police inquiries had already begun – Haigh called at the shop again and accepted an offer of £100 for some of the jewellery. He was paid sixty pounds that day and a further forty pounds on the day after. Mrs Durand-Deacon's sister, on being shown these articles, identified them as her sister's property.

As a result of this evidence, Haigh was asked to go to Chelsea Police Station, and in the evening of February 26, the Divisional Detective Inspector returned from Horsham and saw him. Haigh admitted that the coat and jewellery had belonged to Mrs Durand-Deacon, and when he was asked to give an explanation, said it was a long story and would implicate many people.

Left alone with the inspector, Haigh said coolly, 'Tell me frankly, what are the chances of anyone being released from Broadmoor?'

The inspector declined to discuss this question, and Haigh then said, 'If I told you the truth you wouldn't believe me. It sounds too fantastic for belief.'

The officer immediately cautioned him.

'I understand all that,' said Haigh. 'Mrs Durand-Deacon no longer exists. She has disappeared completely and no trace of her can ever be found. I've destroyed her with acid. You'll find the sludge that remains at Leopold Road. I did the same with the Hendersons and the McSwans. Every trace has gone. How can you prove murder if there's no body?'

Haigh was cautioned again, and then made a long statement which was taken down in writing by the Divisional Detective Inspector. According to this account, Haigh and Mrs Durand-Deacon had gone to Crawley on February 18 in his car, and there in the store he shot her in the back of the head while she was examining some papers supposed to be for use in making artificial finger-nails. Then he made an incision in her throat with a penknife, and collected and drank a glass of her blood. After that he removed her Persian lamb coat and jewellery and put her body in a forty-five-gallon tank. He then went out for tea at a restaurant in Crawley.

After tea, he returned to Leopold Road and with the aid of a stirrup-pump transferred some sulphuric acid from one of the carboys to the tank. Later he had dinner at the George Hotel in Crawley, and then returned to South Kensington. The next day he went to Crawley again and on the way sold Mrs Durand-Deacon's watch at a jeweller's shop in Putney for ten pounds. After having inspected the tank at Leopold Road, he went to the pawnbroker at Horsham with the jewellery and left the Persian lamb coat to be cleaned at Reigate.

On Monday the 21st he returned to Crawley and, finding the body not quite dissolved, emptied out the sludge and pumped some more acid into the tank. Having done this, he again visited the pawnbroker, where he had left the jewellery, receiving sixty pounds that day and a final forty pounds on the next day.

On the 22nd, he found the body of Mrs Durand-Deacon had decomposed, and emptied the sludge outside the store. The only thing not dissolved was her red plastic handbag, and this he tipped out with the sludge.

He said the revolver found in the hat-box was the one with which he had shot Mrs Durand-Deacon. He also added that he had taken a fountain-pen and about thirty shillings in cash from her handbag before he put it in the tank. The crucifix on a chain which she was wearing, and some keys which he had taken from her body, he had pushed into the ground by a hedge in a lane at Buxted. Finally, he gave an account of the murders, between 1944 and 1948, of the three people named McSwan and of Dr and Mrs Henderson.

Up to this point, the inquiries at Crawley had been conducted by the West Sussex Constabulary. The Chief Constable of West Sussex now asked for Scotland Yard assistance, and on March 1 a Chief Inspector of the Metropolitan Police searched the builder's yard and store at Leopold Road. In the store he found a pencil-sharpener, two pieces of red cellophane, a mackintosh, a gas mask and case, a rubber apron and a pair of rubber gloves, some blood-stained whitewash on a wall, and samples from the two carboys which still contained liquid. From the yard he took a bucket and wooden rod, and some earth and sludge.

Later the same day, Haigh's room at the Onslow Court Hotel was searched and a blue shirt was found with what appeared to be bloodstains on the cuffs. When it was shown to Haigh, he admitted the shirt was his and agreed that the blood must be Mrs Durand-Deacon's. All these articles were delivered to the Director of the Laboratory at Scotland Yard. Haigh was then taken to Horsham Police Station and formally charged with the murder of Mrs Durand-Deacon.

The Laboratory experts examined the sludge and earth from the yard at Crawley, and in it found the handle of a red plastic handbag, some false teeth, three gallstones, some fragments of human bone, and a mass of yellow substance resembling melted body fat. Examination of the gallstones showed them to be of the human type; the bones, too, were human and probably those of an elderly woman. The Laboratory also reported the presence of blood on the fur coat, the cuffs of the blue shirt, and on the rubber apron, the gas-mask case, the stained whitewash and a knife found in Haigh's car. There were traces of fat and sulphuric acid on the stirrup-pump and the rubber gloves, as well as on other articles from the yard. The samples taken from the carboys also contained sulphuric acid. The teeth were identified by the dentist who had supplied them to Mrs Durand-Deacon.

On March 1 a card was found in Haigh's hotel room which showed that he had made careful preparation for his crime. On the card were listed, 'drum, enamel, H_2SO_4, a stirrup-pump, gloves, apron, etc.', and certain trade addresses from which, on inquiry, it was established that Haigh had obtained the sulphuric acid and the drum in which he had disposed of the body.

When Haigh's co-director of Hurstlea Products was interviewed, he described how, at Haigh's request, he had removed the leg from one of the stirrup pumps. This was necessary for Haigh's plans, because the pump with the leg attached could not have been inserted into the carboy of acid. Haigh's partner also said that on February 22 Haigh had given him thirty-six pounds in part repayment of a loan of fifty pounds made on February 15. It was on February 22 that Haigh had received sixty pounds from the pawnbroker for some of Mrs Durand-Deacon's jewellery.

Witnesses were found who had seen Haigh driving in Crawley on the evening of February 18, and the book-keeper of the George Hotel remembered a lady, whom she recognised from press photographs as Mrs Durand-Deacon, visiting the hotel for a few minutes between four and five p.m. that day and leaving with Haigh in his car. Haigh had returned to the hotel about nine p.m. and was provided with a towel and soap.

The sale of the dead lady's watch to a Putney jeweller was verified, and on March 8 the keys and the crucifix chain were found, by the aid of a mine detector, under the hedge at Buxted, as Haigh had described.

I had followed the daily unfolding of this fantastic story with a fascinated interest; but, shorn of its trimmings, it was as straightforward a murder case as one could hope for. The arrested man had made a statement, almost every confirmable detail of which had been confirmed. Now, however, into this perfectly straightforward case came a complication, and that complication was the press.

A few days before Haigh's arrest on March 1, newspapers published articles suggesting that he had been responsible, not only for the murder of Mrs Durand-Deacon, but for several other murders. These articles continued on the day after he was charged, when the court had before it only evidence of Haigh's name, age and occupation, and the name of Mrs Durand-Deacon. The press had been strongly advised that publication of anything else at this stage was likely to be contempt of court. Notwithstanding this warning, certain papers published a brief formal report of the police-court proceedings on inside pages while filling their front pages with alleged details of an increasing number of murders laid to Haigh's charge.

On March 4, one newspaper published a report in which it was stated that Scotland Yard was investigating a case in which a vampire murderer drank the blood of his victims. Public protests against publication of such details flowed in to Scotland Yard, as did requests from other newspapers for a confirmation or denial of this story. More important from our point of view, the Legal Department was seriously concerned whether the charge against Haigh of murdering Mrs Durand-Deacon might have been so hopelessly prejudiced that it might have to be dropped altogether.

Fearnley, my Public Information Officer, therefore sent out a confidential memorandum to all newspaper editors through the Press Association, saying that the only statement on this subject had been made to the police under caution, in a case now *sub judice*. The statement might be offered in evidence, and any stories concerning it might prejudge the trial of the accused. He added, with my full approval, the strongly-worded warning, 'The Commissioner wishes to draw the attention of editors to the fact that publication of the contents of that statement or any reference to it would be most improper and would doubtless become a matter for consideration by the court before whom the accused appears.'

Some sections of the press, however, seemed unminded to heed this warning. Soon after midday, Fearnley sent out another memorandum concerning the publication of alleged details in the Henderson and McSwan cases, adding the even stronger note that publication '*will be* a matter for serious consideration by the court.'

Press inquiries continued to be made, and at quarter-past six that evening, we issued a memorandum stating that no further information could be given by the Metropolitan Police.

At nearly midnight, Fearnley telephoned me at a public dinner to say that he had felt it necessary to take the unusual course of issuing a memorandum to editors in my name, stating categorically, 'I feel that further speculation on the whereabouts of various missing persons currently mentioned in the press would not be in the public interest. Any developments in these cases will be officially reported by Scotland Yard through the usual channels.'

This, at last, had some effect. The press quietened down before irreparable damage had been done; though it remains to be said that one newspaper editor did appear before the Lord Chief Justice for contempt of court, and was sent to prison for three months.

Haigh himself was tried at the Sussex Assizes before Mr Justice Humphreys on July 18, and after a trial lasting two days was found guilty and sentenced to death.

The defence admitted the killing of Mrs Durand-Deacon, but sought to show that Haigh was insane at the time. The only witness for the defence was a psychiatrist who contended that Haigh suffered from delusions of grandeur and that he did not think Haigh knew he was doing wrong when he killed Mrs Durand-Deacon. But under cross-examination he agreed that when committing the crime, Haigh must have believed that he was punishable by law. In view of this admission the Attorney-General did not think it necessary to call any evidence in rebuttal.

In addition to the murder of Mrs Durand-Deacon, Haigh confessed to the murders of Donald McSwan in 1944, and his parents, Donald and Amy McSwan, in 1945, in the basement of a house in Gloucester Road. He also admitted the killing of Dr and Mrs Archibald Henderson at Crawley, in 1948, and stated that he had disposed of their bodies in the same way as that of Mrs Durand-Deacon. Inquiries confirmed these confessions and established that his motive had been one of gain. By a series of forged receipts and powers of attorney he had obtained possession of the houses, investments and bank balances of his victims, and he had sold their personal property in Horsham and elsewhere. Some of this property was traced and identified, and other possessions of theirs were found in Haigh's room at the Onslow Court Hotel. He had been careful to choose as his victims persons with few friends or relatives. Such as there were, he put off by forged messages and letters to explain the absence of his victims and his authority to conduct their affairs.

It may seem extraordinary, but in spite of occasional doubts, no relatives or friends of the dead men and women had ever reported their suspicions to the police, and if Haigh's own confidence had not led to his undoing in the case of Mrs Durand-Deacon, the disappearance of these five persons might never have come to light. Haigh, indeed, boasted that he had similarly disposed of three other persons, but careful inquiries showed that there was no reason to believe this.

In the Haigh case, and in other notable cases during my Commissionership, the judges' rules governing legal insanity, known as the M'Naghten Rules, came under criticism. It is often urged that a man must be insane to commit murders of the kind done by Haigh, Heath and Christie, and in the Haigh case particularly, the fact that he took no pains to avoid leaving a series of clues that could hardly be overlooked has been adduced as evidence of his abnormality. But abnormality is not the same thing as insanity; for who among us is absolutely normal? And if it is said that no sane man would leave such obvious clues to his misdeeds, it must be remembered that criminals guilty of less serious crimes, on whose behalf nobody advances a plea of insanity, do exactly this. That is why they are caught.

The M'Naghten Rules have the great advantage that they are simple and easy for a jury to understand. It is possible to produce evidence to show that a prisoner knew what he was doing and that what he was doing was wrong, and these are questions that can properly be put to a jury. It would be quite otherwise if the defence of irresistible impulse were admitted, for who can say that an impulse was irresistible? All that is certain is that the prisoner did not resist it, and the views of the most eminent psychologists on this question can be no more than opinions. When experts disagree, how is a jury to judge between them? Moreover, the fate of the prisoner is not finally settled by this verdict of the jury. Every death sentence is reviewed by the Home Secretary with the help of his advisers, and every factor, whether it be the circumstances of the crime or the mental state of the prisoner, is taken into account before a final decision is taken either to let the sentence stand or to recommend a reprieve.

This procedure, though it may be illogical – and who ever thought of accusing the English of being logical! – has the great merit of many English institutions, that it works and works uncommonly well. In the present state of our knowledge, I think it would be wise to hesitate a long time before introducing any change.

In my evidence before the Royal Commission on Capital Punishment I suggested that, as in the Indian Penal Code, the judge should have discretion, when a verdict of murder is found, to pass either the death sentence or a sentence of life imprisonment. The Commission did not like the proposal, and in their report suggested instead that such discretion should be given to the jury. The suggestion has been widely criticised, I think rightly, as introducing a new concept into English law. An English jury has always been regarded as a body whose duty it is to pronounce on fact. For this, an assembly of twelve good men and true is an admirable instrument. But even on this limited issue juries have been known to be swayed by sentimental considerations, and on the question of sentence there would be a real risk that their verdict would reflect their emotions rather than their judgement.

A judge is, or should be, immune from any such weakness, and I find it hard to understand the argument that the burden of decision which has been carried for years by successive Home Secretaries is too great to be borne by a judge of the High Court, especially as the Prerogative of Mercy will still remain to be employed in any case where there is ground for clemency.

Chapter 6
THE CRIMINAL
INVESTIGATION DEPARTMENT

THE fame, all over the world, of Scotland Yard as a detective agency is so great that it came as a surprise to me when I discovered how small a part of the Metropolitan Police is represented by the Criminal Investigation Department. In an establishment of 20,000 men it numbers only 1,400 – a mere handful of men to cope with the crime of the Metropolis. So important are they, however, that in spite of our shortage of men I kept them up to strength and indeed increased their number by two hundred.

C.I.D. officers are to be found not only at Scotland Yard; they are distributed, under the Divisional Detective Inspector, to every division of the Metropolitan Police District. At Central Office (or C.1) there is a picked group of senior detectives under a Chief Superintendent, who are always available to undertake the more important and difficult inquiries, whether in London or in the provinces. It is generally one of these Central Office detectives, whose names are better known to the public than the Commissioner's, who figure in the newspaper headlines attached to some sensational case: 'Scotland Yard Called In'.

All Chief Constables of provincial police forces have their own C.I.D. and are, of course, completely independent of Scotland Yard, but from time to time they ask for the assistance of an officer from the Yard, recognising that he will have had far greater opportunities of gaining experience than the officer in a county or borough force. Such help is always freely given and generously recognised. If there was at one time something in the nature of a feud between the provincial police and the Mets, as they are called, it has now ceased to be of any importance. Such a feud was in any event stupid, for unless all forces work together, the only person to benefit is the criminal. I always sought to encourage understanding and co-operation between the Mets and the provincial forces, and in this I was greatly helped by the attitude of the Chief Constables, and by the mingling at the Police College of members of forces from all over the country. There is no doubt that today there is a greater readiness to work together than ever before.

The C.I.D. itself is very like a university, and provides a wonderful medium of education for any young man able to take advantage of it. The C.I.D. officer quickly acquires a wider general knowledge than most people, and the senior officers of the branch accumulate during their service a great amount of information about all sides of life, and the ability to mix on easy terms with all types of people. They become, perhaps, a little sceptical; but none, in my experience, has lost his belief in human nature. They are quick to scent a bad story; but equally quick to recognise a true one, however unlikely it may seem.

It is naturally the ambition of many police recruits to enter the C.I.D., but there is no direct entry and every recruit begins by two years' duty on the beat in uniform. If he shows aptitude for detective work he may be appointed an aide to the C.I.D. He puts off his uniform and is attached to regular C.I.D. officers in his division, where, while he gains practical experience of detective work, his fitness for it can be judged. If he is found suitable, he is sent after a year or so to a Selection Board at headquarters, and if he is selected, joins the C.I.D. For twelve months he is on probation, and early in this period is sent to the Detective Training School at Hendon for a ten-weeks' course. Finally he sits for an examination, and if he is successful is appointed as a member of what its officers, with a pardonable emphasis on the first word, call 'the department'.

Henceforward his life will be very different from that of his uniformed colleagues. He may be posted at headquarters either in the Central Office or in one of the specialist departments such as the Criminal Record Office or Fingerprint Registry, or he may go to one of the divisions outside.

Shift duty is for him a thing of the past, but his hours will be limited only by the requirements of his work. He will get no time off or payment on account of overtime, but only a fixed detective allowance to compensate him for long and irregular hours. His real reward is to have entered on a life which by common consent is of absorbing interest and variety. He is likely to find himself spending many weary weeks tracking an epidemic of bicycle-lamp stealing from a factory cycle store. On the other hand he may be plunged into such a case as that which became known as the Battle of Heath Row. It is worth describing as an example of the wide discretion allowed to a divisional detective inspector to 'run his own show'. In press reports at the time, indeed, its success was attributed to the Flying Squad, who are to the divisional C.I.D. what the C.I.D. are to the man on the beat: objects of a certain friendly envy. The Flying Squad certainly gave valuable assistance, but the Battle of Heath Row was first and foremost a victory for a Divisional Detective Inspector and the men under his command.

About the middle of July, 1948, information was received by Divisional Detective Inspector Roberts of 'T' Division that a gang of dangerous criminals had made a plan to raid the bonded warehouse at London Airport where goods to a very high value are always in store. The plan was to drug the canteen tea of the British Overseas Airways Corporation staff in charge of the warehouse and then carry off the contents, using force if necessary.

An experienced Chief Inspector of the C.I.D. is expected to be quite capable of carrying the load of such a case himself. Roberts reported to his Chief Superintendent, and was told to make the dispositions he thought necessary. Realising that he had not sufficient resources in his own division to deal with a raid of this size, he asked for the help of the Flying Squad, and at a meeting of representatives of the police and B.O.A.C., a plan of action to counter the attack was prepared.

The raid, Roberts learned, was planned for the night of July 28-29, when a consignment of a million dollars' worth of bullion was due to arrive by air. Apart from this, there were already goods in store worth about £500,000. The store was a converted hangar standing about eighty yards inside the airport, opposite the main entrance from the Bath Road, and entry to it was by two large sliding doors in one of which was a small wicket gate.

Shortly after ten p.m. on the night of the raid, police officers assembled in another part of the airport and were divided into two parties, one to go inside the hangar, the other to remain outside. The first party of ten, concealed in a van belonging to B.O.A.C., was taken to the store. It included three officers who had volunteered to take the place of the B.O.A.C. security officer and the two loaders who would otherwise have been on duty in the warehouse that night. Dressed in the appropriate

B.O.A.C. uniform, their part was to behave as though under the influence of drugs when the arrival of the raiders was signalled, and to risk any consequences that such a role might entail. The remaining seven officers concealed themselves at various points within the warehouse and awaited the thieves.

Outside the warehouse and about twenty yards away, other officers were concealed in another B.O.A.C. van with instructions, if any unauthorized vehicles backed to the gates of the warehouse, to reverse their van up to it so as to prevent its getting away. They were then to assist in arresting the occupants if they tried to escape. Other police vehicles were posted at strategic points around the airport to intercept any stolen cars or lorries the thieves might seize in an effort to get away.

By half-past eleven the police forces were all in position. The minutes ticked away with a mounting tension which can be imagined, until just before one o'clock a large, covered van drove into the airport and backed up against the bonded warehouse. Seven men, all masked and armed with bludgeons, went towards the warehouse, while the driver, dressed in blue dungarees and wearing a B.O.A.C. cap, took up his position at the door, armed with a starting-handle.

The officers waiting inside saw two masked men come in, who, after a quick look round, left and returned almost at once with five other men. One was carrying an iron bar while the rest were armed with bludgeons. All were wearing gloves or socks on their hands. Two men went into the office, where they found the three police officers dressed in B.O.A.C. uniform, breathing stertorously as if they had indeed drunk the drugged tea. With great coolness, the officers continued to feign unconsciousness while the thieves bound them with pieces of rope and placed adhesive tape across their mouths. One officer, no doubt to see if he was really unconscious, was struck or kicked violently on the back of the head. Despite his pain, he did not give away the fact that he was shamming. Having disposed of the three officers and stolen the keys of the safe from them, the two thieves came out of the office and handed the keys to another man, who tried them in the safe lock.

At this point Chief Inspector Lee, of the Flying Squad, decided the time for action had come. He shouted, 'We are police of the Flying Squad. Stay where you are.' Three officers ran to the door to cut off any escape, and the others converged on the gang. There was a shout from the thieves of 'Kill the bastards! Get the guns!' and a wild mêlée followed, the police using their truncheons and the thieves their bludgeons, a spanner and a large pair of boltcutters.

Lee tackled the man who appeared to be the ringleader of the gang, was hit on the head with an iron bar, and carried bodily through the door of the warehouse. The struggle continued outside, and the ringleader was seen to throw the safe keys on the ground before he was captured. Four other members of the gang were engaged by other policemen and after a violent struggle were overpowered. Their companions managed to get through the door, but outside they and the driver of their van found the second party of officers waiting for them. One man threatened the police with a gun, while two others, after temporarily sheltering under the van, came out and fought with a bludgeon, a broken bottle and the starting handle, until they, too, were arrested.

The eight prisoners were then taken to Harlington Police Station and charged. They made no reply except that one, Smith, said he would kill the man who had given them away. They had all been hit on the head by police truncheons and needed to be stitched up, while nine of the police had been injured, mostly severe bruises on the head and limbs. One had a fractured nose, one a cut on his right hip and leg caused by a broken bottle.

The police had learned that a loader employed at the airport had given the gang information which enabled them to plan their raid, and he was therefore brought in and interrogated. At first he denied any knowledge of the affair, but later admitted he had given information to the gang and was to be rewarded after the theft had been successfully carried out. The members of the gang were paraded before him, and he picked out four of them as the men with whom he had been in touch.

The prisoners eventually stood their trial at the Central Criminal Court, and were sentenced to periods of penal servitude varying from five to twelve years, with the exception of the loader, who was bound over in his own recognisance of ten pounds for two years. He was a tool who, having met some of the gang in public houses and been treated to drinks, was gradually induced to give a little information. He was then threatened with exposure to the police unless he went on to give full details of the arrangements in the warehouse which enabled the gang to plan their coup.

To complete the story, it must be added that, after all, the aeroplane which was to have brought in the million dollars' worth of bullion was held up by fog and did not fly in until the following day!

The Heath Row case, extraordinary in the ambitious nature of the intended coup, is more exciting than the majority of C.I.D. cases. The recruit soon discovers that the popular idea of a detective as one who solves his problems by brilliant deductions or flashes of intuition bears little resemblance to the truth. On the contrary, he will learn the justice of the comment by an experienced member of the department that ninety-five per cent. of successful detection depends on perspiration, three per cent. on inspiration, and two per cent. on luck. Above all he will need to develop his powers of observation and a curiosity about every human activity, and to form a rapid and trustworthy judgement of the character and propensities of all sorts of men. He must meet criminals and get to know them and their habits and places of resort, and all the time he must be on his guard against the temptations which, for their own ends, they will spread before him. These temptations are very real, and from time to time lead to the downfall of a promising young detective; but what is surprising is not the occasional lapse, but that there are even more cases like that of the detective sergeant, whose pay was about eight pounds a week, and who unhesitatingly reported to his superiors that he had been offered £3,000 to close his eyes to certain criminal activities.

The good detective is at once a good workman and an artist. It is no uncommon thing in an inquiry for an officer to interview hundreds, even thousands of persons. Most of them will be unable to tell him anything of value, but there is always the possibility that among them will be one or two who have seen or heard something which throws light on the case.

One case which most impressed me was that of the little girl who was found murdered in Windsor Great Park. There had been a fair that day, and the detectives sought out every person who had been to the fair. They collected snapshots taken by various visitors, enlarging the portraits of every person in the picture and seeking out the people shown. Everyone who had been in the field where the body was found was at length identified and seen. One couple sitting by the river had seen somebody pass. A passer-by had seen yet another visitor, and so little by little the comings and going in that field were reconstructed so vividly that one could almost imagine a film had been taken of the scene for hours on end.

An even more striking case was that of the little girl who was taken from a hospital in Blackburn and brutally murdered by being bashed against a wall. The only clue was a bottle on which were found some fingerprints. Comparison with those in the great collection at Scotland Yard showed that the owner was unknown to the police, and when after the fullest inquiry no further progress could be made, the officers in charge of the case decided there was nothing for it but to take the prints of every man in Blackburn, a town of over 100,000 inhabitants. A promise was given, and kept, that the prints of all innocent persons would be destroyed, and the officers embarked on their task of taking prints from all the male inhabitants. Those who had left the district were traced, even though some had gone abroad. The task went on for about three months, and eventually, among the 46,253 prints taken, a set was found corresponding to those on the bottle.

'Patience and perseverance made a Bishop of his Reverence,' and the C.I.D. officer must cultivate similar virtues. No possible line of inquiry must be ignored, no detail must be dismissed as unimportant. This was never better illustrated than in the investigation into the murder of Miss Curran in Northern Ireland. In this case Superintendent Capstick and his helpers interviewed 40,000 people before they were able eventually to arrest a young airman who was found guilty but insane. Utter confusion will ensue unless such a mass of material is handled in a most methodical manner. Every statement must be indexed in such a way that it can be turned up at a moment's notice. Sir Richard Pim, the Inspector-General of the Ulster Constabulary, told me when the case was finished how greatly he and his officers had been impressed by the patience and method of the Yard officers.

Even when the original inquiry into a case proves fruitless, the department does not abandon hope. The record remains on the files, but more important still, it remains in the minds of the officers concerned. In 1949, a policeman was violently assaulted with an iron bar in Sloane Street and nearly killed. Only two of his three assailants were arrested, but two years afterwards, a hint of the whereabouts of the third man was sufficient for an officer who had been engaged on the case, and an arrest followed at once.

The good detective must master the art of interrogation, and the first essential is to gather all possible information about the crime before beginning the interrogation. The second is to understand the character of the person interrogated and to act accordingly. The method will vary according to the temperament and personality of the investigator. One will draw the witness out by his frank and friendly interest in all manner of things not even remotely connected with the crime. Another, by unanswerable logic, will force the witness back from one line of defence to another, until at last the hopelessness of further untruths is obvious. Many detectives, finding criminals eager to share the burden of their secret, believe that a paternal manner, a cup of tea and a cigarette work greater wonders than any form of browbeating.

What the detective must not do is to adopt methods which savour of violence or the 'third degree'. So far from using such methods, he is in fact closely limited by the necessity of observing the Judges' Rules. These lay down that once a police officer has made up his mind to charge a person with a crime, he must caution him before asking any more questions, and the same applies to the questioning of a person in custody.

The caution should be in these terms: 'Do you wish to say anything in answer to this charge? You are not obliged to say anything unless you wish to do so, but whatever you say will be taken down in writing and may be used as evidence.' Not, it will be noted, 'in evidence *against* you', for the statement may, in fact, serve to exonerate the prisoner.

This rule was made for the protection of prisoners, and though it may from time to time cramp the style of the investigating officer, it is recognised by the police as a good and necessary rule and I doubt if it often or seriously interferes with the conduct of an inquiry.

In the trial of Alfred Charles Whiteway, the defence rested its entire case on an attack upon the statement made by Whiteway to the police. This attack carried no weight with the jury, but it did lead to suggestions that the police should use tape recorders when taking statements in important cases. I do not think that those who made this suggestion realise the difficulties involved. A great many instruments would be needed to take all police statements, and even if these were available at the right place and at the right time, there would still be the possibility of an accusation that the recording had been interfered with, that it did not cover everything which had occurred between the arrested man and the police, or, as a last resort, that it was not a recording of the accused's voice at all. In the majority of cases there is never any question of what the accused did say, and the introduction of expensive and to some extent unwieldy mechanical equipment instead of pen, ink and paper, seems to me to create as many difficulties as it solves.

If the detective is to gather all available information before he tackles his suspect he must cultivate the habit of exact observation, even of the apparently insignificant detail. Chief Superintendent F. R. Cherrill, who retired after thirty-eight years' service from the position of head of the Finger-print Department, tells a story that illustrates the value of continued alertness in observation. A prisoner was charged with burglary, and part of the evidence against him was a print of an index finger left at the scene of the crime. As usual, enlarged photographs of this print, and of a similar one taken from the register at Scotland Yard, were produced in court, and Cherrill gave evidence of their identity.

Defending counsel asked, 'What are the lines across these two prints?'

'No doubt they're the result of a cut or scar on the finger,' Cherrill answered.

Counsel then asked his client to show his finger to the jury. The prisoner licked his finger, wiped it on his trousers to remove the grime, and showed it to the jury. They inspected the finger and shook their heads. The judge asked to see it, and having inspected it said, 'I can see no scar on this finger, Mr Cherrill.'

'No, my lord,' said Cherrill, unabashed. 'But the print is of the index finger of the left hand, and the prisoner has shown you his right.'

When the prisoner reluctantly showed his left hand, there was the tell-tale scar.

But observation, however keen and accurate, will not always suffice. Often the detective has no point of departure in his inquiry, and it is then that his contacts with the underworld become of the first importance. Many a detective's evidence begins with the words. 'Acting on information received . . .', and if anyone were tactless enough to ask him where that information was received from, he would imitate the tactics of the Flying Squad officer who was giving evidence about a suspect he had followed in one of the Squad's disguised 'Q' cars,

'What sort of a car was it, officer?' the magistrate asked.

'It was a car, sir,' replied the officer with the utmost respect, but with unbending will.

Nor could further questions budge him. It is not in the public interest that 'Q' cars should be described in open court, and it is not in the public interest that the detective should give away his contacts in the underworld who, often at risk to themselves, supply the information upon which the police act. The motives of these sources of 'information received' are, I suppose, as many and as mixed as the informants themselves. Some do it for money. Some act for motives of jealousy, revenge or spite. It is a tribute to the C.I.D. that quite a number are moved by gratitude to a detective who has helped them over a sticky patch.

Having completed his inquiry, the detective's duty is far from complete. He produces a report to which are attached the verbatim statements of all the essential witnesses. I have read hundreds of these reports in the last forty years and I never cease to admire the way in which they are compiled. Clear and logical, they marshal the facts in order; nothing is omitted, nothing is exaggerated; comment is kept to a minimum and personal views and prejudices are entirely absent. They are models of what a report should be. The detective's report is the basis of the proceedings in the criminal court and here he is often one of the principal witnesses. On his ability as a witness much depends. Long training and experience have taught him to give his evidence clearly and fairly and to bear with patience the hostile and often very subtle assaults of defending counsel.

Sometimes criticism of police evidence in court rebounds on the critic, as for instance when counsel ridiculed the evidence of two officers who stated that the prisoner had said he 'proceeded' from A to B.

'"Proceed" is a police word,' said counsel, 'and obviously not one likely to have been used by the prisoner.'

But the officers stuck to their guns and persisted that 'proceeded' was the word used.

Later the prisoner gave evidence and was cross-examined. 'I proceeded . . .' he said. It turned out that he was an old lag, who had heard the word used in court so often that he had adopted it as his own.

The detectives of the Central Office of the C.I.D. usually come to public notice on account of their part in some sensational murder case. But these form only a fraction of the crime picture. Less well known, but even more valuable, is the C.I.D.'s work on other types of crime involving painstaking inquiry over many months or even years. A particular case of this kind illustrates the immense amount of work that must be done before a prosecution can be launched.

Towards the end of 1950, it became known to the Board of Trade that a vast conspiracy in which many persons were engaged had been going on from 1947 to 1950. As a result, large quantities of decorated china had been diverted from export to the home market. Under the control of a man who himself remained in the background, twelve people trading under a variety of names had obtained and sold in the home market china and earthenware to the value of at least £66,000, though the transactions no doubt amounted to a far higher sum. The Board of Trade asked for the assistance of Scotland Yard, and a Chief Inspector and a detective constable were instructed to undertake the inquiry. For three years they laboured to unravel the threads of this conspiracy, travelling all over the country to interview witnesses, and to examine books, invoices and correspondence. Nine thousand documents were photographed and a report of nearly 200 pages was submitted to the Board of Trade.

The method employed by the conspirators, under cover of an export licence from the Board, was to order quantities of china and earthenware, giving a written guarantee to the manufacturers that the goods were intended for export. At the same time they gave instructions for the goods to be crated, marked with detailed shipping marks and delivered to various London wharves for shipment. There was no intention to ship the goods abroad and they often arrived at the wharf after the ship named had already sailed. Instead, the goods were collected by carriers, who came with instructions from the conspirators and invoices bearing the names and addresses of fictitious firms and false export reject numbers. In this way they reached retailers all over the country.

As a result of our three-year investigation, twelve defendants and two firms were charged at Bow Street with conspiracy and contravention of the relevant orders. Seldom can a group of such clever rogues have been brought into the dock. All but one had received a public school education and one was a Bachelor of Law. Five had criminal records. They were defended by three Queen's Counsel and seventeen juniors, and the proceedings at Bow Street and the Old Bailey last for sixty-nine days. The Old Bailey trial lasted forty-one days – one of the longest in the history of the court. During all this time nothing shook the evidence of the Chief Inspector and his assistant, and they had the satisfaction of seeing all but two of the prisoners convicted and sentenced to periods of imprisonment ranging from nine months to five years. The accused were also ordered to pay costs amounting in all to £15,250.

At the end of the case the judge, Mr Justice Glyn Jones, specially commended the officers for their admirable work in preparing the case and for the way in which they gave evidence in the witness box.

So far I have written of the detective as though he worked alone or with only a colleague in his inquiry, but of course behind him stands the machine at Scotland Yard to which he can and will refer at every stage of his inquiry. There are at the Yard three departments which have become indispensable to the detective: the Criminal Record Office, the Fingerprint Department, and the Forensic Science Laboratory. Each of these remarkable institutions deserves detailed description.

Chapter 7
THE CRIMINAL RECORD OFFICE

THE Criminal Record Office, though staffed by Metro-politan Police and housed at Scotland Yard, is national in character. It contains complete records of all persons convicted of serious crime in Great Britain, and provides information for police forces throughout the country. Most countries have some centralised system or systems of criminal records, and C.R.O. is in touch with these national offices all over the world. It is thus both a national and an international registry of crimes, a 'Who's Who' of their perpetrators, a means of enabling new crimes to be traced to old criminals, several crimes to be traced to the same person, and old criminals to be recognised with certainty when they are rearrested.

Each record consists of the name, age and personal descrip-tion of the criminal, a photograph, and a list of his offences and sentences. Whenever a criminal comes into police custody anywhere in Great Britain, a form with his description and fingerprints is sent to the Criminal Record Office. Any previous convictions which he admits are checked, and even if none is admitted, a search is still made, so that if there are any previous convictions, they can be linked up. There are over two and a half million cards in the Criminal Record Office, and in view of the great number of aliases adopted by some criminals, there may be as many as forty or fifty cards for one offender. The record is held by a man with 440.

Proof of previous convictions is necessary to enable a court to decide on the appropriate sentence after an offender has been convicted. Until the passing of the Criminal Justice Act, 1948, this involved the attendance of officers in court to give evidence of identity. Under the new Act, a certificate by the Commissioner of Police of the Metropolis is admissible as evi-dence of a man's criminal record, and while this has thrown a heavy additional task on the Criminal Record Office, it has resulted in a very considerable saving of police time in attend-ance at Court.

In addition to the main collection of criminal records, there are a number of supplementary indices, each of great value. The most interesting is the *Modus Operandi* Index. This is based on the fact that criminals are creatures of habit and are apt, once a particular method has proved successful, to go on repeating it. Oddly enough, even after several detections and arrests, some offenders go on repeating themselves and seem either too lazy or too stupid to vary their methods, which is fortunate for the police.

The index consists of cards on which are entered information about all important criminals who employ a definite method in committing their crimes. It consists of a number of sections. In the Nominal Section there is a separate card giving the name and every alias known to have been used by the criminal, the year of his birth, and his height. These three particulars are enough to allow a quick selection of probable cards which can then be further winnowed by following cross-references on each card to more detailed records.

In the Method Section the methods employed by criminals are recorded in alphabetical order, beginning with Abduction, Arson, Assault, Baby Farming, and so on down to Treason, Warehousebreaking and White Slave Traffic. Each card is filed under the appropriate heading according to the year of birth and height of the offender. Under some headings the number of cards is very great, so for easy reference the heading is subdivided. For example, Fraud is by far the largest section, and this is further subdivided:

The character assumed in committing the fraud
The medium used
The class of person defrauded
The kind of property obtained
Special forms of fraud

Each of these classes is subdivided still further. Under 'Character assumed', the headings read Actor, Agent (with seven sub-headings), Airman, Architect, through Foreign Prince, Freemason, down to Veterinary Surgeon, Wealthy Person and Woman (Man Posing As).

Under 'Medium used', the headings read: Business (with many sub-headings); Documents (begging letter, betting tickets, bills, billhead, cheques, down to pawn tickets); Goods (carpets, furs, clothes, jewellery, down to 'water as whisky' and

77

'wine').

Under 'Class of person defrauded', the headings read: Actor, Agent, Antique Dealer, through Clergyman, Executor, M.P., Officials (Bank, Inland Revenue, etc.) to Women.

The next heading, 'Kind of Property Obtained', is self-explanatory. The fifth, 'Special Forms of Fraud', ranges from Answering Advertisements, Fortune Telling, Gold Bar Trick and Share-pushing, to Tea Selling and Wallet or Purse Lost.

The Fraud Index is, indeed, a sad epitome of the gullibility, as well as the misplaced ingenuity, of the human race.

For one offender there may be several cards: a main card indexed under the most important type of crime in which he has been concerned, and a subsidiary card for every classification under which his method of working can be brought. A man who specialises in fraud, for example, would have a main card under Fraud, and if he generally poses as an Actor, uses the Begging Letter, defrauds Clergymen, and obtains money on an allegation that his Car Had Broken Down, subsidiary cards would be placed in the Fraud Section under these sub-headings.

A third section of the *Modus Operandi* Index records any outstanding deformity of a criminal, whether or not he is recorded in the Method Section. Deformity is interpreted in a wide sense to cover any characteristic feature, and the cards are arranged alphabetically according to parts of the body, for example Cheek (birthmark, dimple, mole, wart or scar), or Eyes (blind, cast, crossed or squint, defective, missing or glass, protruding, etc.), in each case distinguishing left or right. There are similar cards for Chin, Nose, and other parts of the body, and for Speech (accent, lisp, stammer, etc.).

The sections for Tattoo Marks and Nicknames need no explanation. That for Characteristic Peculiarities begins with Accompanied by Children, or by Dog, and proceeds by way of Bites Finger Nails, Boots or Shoes Taken Off (in which category the famous Flannelfoot held pride of place), Feigns Illness, down to Suffers From (in the cases of those who love to discuss their ailments) and When Speaking (rubs nose, gesticulates, or exhibits some habitual movement).

If a person recorded in the Index is sentenced to over six months' imprisonment, all cards relating to him are removed to a Suspense Section while he is 'inside', in order to relieve the live index of useless cards.

Even if a criminal is sufficiently wary to vary his methods, he seldom does so completely. If, for example, his usual offence is fraud and his method is to impersonate a solicitor's clerk, he may decide to change his role to that of a journalist, but he will probably continue to prey on clergymen or women, and to extract bogus fees or subscriptions, and he will find it difficult to disguise his age, height and various personal deformities or pecularities.

Not the least remarkable thing about the Criminal Record Office is the immense amount of knowledge carried in the heads of the officers working there. As soon as a crime is reported, they are usually able, without looking at their cards, to name several 'likely starters'. Some of these can be eliminated at once because a reference to their cards shows that they are already in custody. Other suspects whose names are forwarded to the divisional C.I.D. may be able to produce a satisfactory alibi. The remainder are given very close scrutiny by divisional detectives, and with luck evidence may be brought to light linking one of them with the crime.

If the criminal has been seen, a description will probably have been sent in to C.R.O., though, since most witnesses are far from being trained observers, there will often be a variation in their descriptions that is at once amazing and baffling. One will have seen a short, fat man in a brown coat, another a tallish man in grey. But often there will be some feature which has caught the observer's attention – a limp, a squint, a stammer, a foreign or north country accent, a cauliflower ear or a broken nose, loquacity or taciturnity, ginger hair or a bald head. Armed with this information, the detective is able to weed out his list of suspects still further, and arrive at a short list which will repay investigation.

An example of the help which the Criminal Record Office can give to detectives at the start of an investigation was the case of Neville Heath. On June 21, 1946, a chambermaid at the Pembridge Court Hotel in Bayswater entered a bedroom that had been occupied for the past four or five days by a couple who had described themselves as Lieutenant-Colonel and Mrs N. G. C. Heath. The girl was horrified to find on the bed the dead body of a woman. The ankles were tied tightly together with a handkerchief and her body, which was horribly mutilated, bore the marks of teeth and flagellation. The doctor soon established that the woman's death was due to suffocation. Detectives making their usual systematic search of the room found a single fingerprint on the washbasin, though it had evidently been scoured to remove any marks.

A search of the files of C.R.O. brought to light a card for Neville George Clevely Heath, born in 1917, who after a period in a Borstal Institution for larceny, housebreaking, and false pretences, had joined the Royal Air Force. He had been dismissed from the R.A..F. after conviction by court-martial of a number of offences, and had a later conviction for posing as a lieutenant-colonel and wearing decorations to which he was not entitled. Comparison of the fingerprint found on the washbasin with this man's recorded print confirmed that he was indeed the Heath we were looking for. Detectives, instead of seeking 'a man', were now seeking a man whose description and characteristics they knew; and this within a few hours of the crime having been discovered.

Heath's home was visited and kept under observation, but he did not return to it. Inquiries were made at all the hotels, clubs and public houses which he was known to frequent, as well as at many others in West London where there was an off-chance that he might have been seen. All his known associates were interviewed, again with no result.

A sure source of information for the police in many cases is the London taxi-driver. The usual inquiries were made among them, and one was found who remembered that at about midnight on the night of the murder, he had driven a dark girl and a man answering Heath's description from a club in South Kensington to the Pembridge Court Hotel. The night-club receptionist was interviewed, and both she and the taxi-driver were able to give a good description of the couple, though the man was known to the receptionist by the name of Armstrong. The murdered girl was identified as Mrs Margery Gardner.

At this point occurred the first of Heath's surprising actions in this surprising case. He wrote to Scotland Yard saying that he had given the key of his bedroom at the Pembridge Court Hotel to Mrs Gardner, who intended to receive a man friend. When he returned to the hotel he found Mrs Gardner dead, but was too scared to tell the police because he himself was wanted for fraud. He gave a detailed description of the man whom he said had been with Mrs Gardner. He also said he was sending the whip with which she had been flogged, which he had found in the bedroom when he returned to it. The whip, however, never arrived.

A description of Heath had, of course, been circulated throughout the country, as a result of which we received from the Worthing police a report that he had been seen there. Through a wartime acquaintance of Heath's, the investigating officer learned that Heath had gone to Worthing to visit a girl with whom he had previously been friendly. She was interviewed, and said that Heath had told her a murder had been committed in his room at a London hotel, and that he had informed the police. The girl's parents viewed his story with considerable alarm, and as soon as he heard of their attitude he disappeared.

The case had reached this stage when to my room came Howe, head of the Criminal Investigation Department, and Fearnley, my Public Information Officer. Fearnley had learned that a photograph of Heath was in the possession of a daily newspaper, which proposed to publish it. The Commissioner has no power to prevent a newspaper from publishing what it pleases, subject to proceedings for contempt of court, but he can, and does, give advice on matters where the public interest is involved. Howe pointed out that the only evidence connecting Heath with the Pembridge Court Hotel on the night of the murder was that of the taxi-driver and, to a lesser extent, of the night-club receptionist. They were both prepared to identify Heath. But if a photograph were published, the defence might be able to cast doubt on their vital evidence and say that they were influenced by the picture they had seen in the press. The prosecution might fail as a result. Howe therefore strongly urged me to advise against publication.

It was a difficult decision to take. We had no reason to suppose at that time that Heath would commit further murders, but there was always the chance that he might, and then we should be accused of having deprived some unfortunate girl of her only means of knowing that she was associating with a murderer. Nevertheless, I was convinced that Howe was right. I took the responsibility of advising the press not to publish any photographs, and the press complied.

On July 3, a young ex-Wren named Doreen Marshall, who was staying at the Norfolk Hotel, Bournemouth, went to dinner with another resident calling himself Group Captain Rupert Brooke. After dinner they left the hotel together, but the night porter did not see Brooke return. When he mentioned this next day, Brooke laughed the matter off, saying he had taken a ladder and climbed into his room by the window as a joke. As Miss Marshall did not return, however, the manager became anxious and asked Brooke about her. He treated the inquiry lightly, but said he would go to the police and give them any help he could. He did so, and at the police station identified a photograph of the girl, whom he said he had left near the pier at half-past twelve. He had understood she was going back to the hotel.

Brooke's story was glib, but he had reckoned without the memory for faces that is part of a good detective's equipment. The detective constable at Bournemouth to whom he told his story felt sure that he had seen Brooke's face before. He remembered the photograph of the man Heath, which had been circulated in the *Police Gazette,* and decided to telephone Scotland Yard. At the request of the Yard officers, Brooke, protesting strongly, was detained. As he was dressed only in sports shirt and flannels, he asked to be allowed to go back to his hotel to collect a coat. The police, however, collected it for him, and found in the pocket a cloakroom ticket issued at Bournemouth West Station. They went there and recovered a suitcase, the contents of which were fatal for Brooke. In it were a heavy whip, a blue woollen scarf and, in a jacket pocket, a single imitation pearl. There were no fingerprints or marks on the whip, but examination in the Laboratory at Scotland Yard showed the scarf to be stained with blood of the same group as that of the murdered Mrs Gardner.

On this evidence, Scotland Yard officers brought Brooke back to London, where at an identification parade he was picked out by the taxi-driver who had taken him to the Pembridge Court Hotel, and by the night-club receptionist. Faced with this, he acknowledged his identity and was charged with the murder of Mrs Gardner.

Meanwhile, Bournemouth police intensified their search for the missing Doreen Marshall. A girl out with her dog in Branksome Chine noticed a swarm of flies, suspected what was attracting them, and ran to the police. They found the body of Doreen Marshall, naked but for one shoe, partly hidden under a rhododendron bush. Nearby were twenty-seven imitation pearls identical with the one found in 'Brooke's' jacket pocket. They also found that 'Group Captain Brooke' had pawned a ring for five pounds and sold a crystal fob watch for three pounds. Both of these had belonged to Miss Marshall.

I have generally been too busy during my working life to attend many criminal trials, but I had not been long at Scotland Yard when Heath was tried, and I decided that it would be a useful thing to witness at length at least one important case. The Heath whom I saw at the Old Bailey seemed to me a very collected, self-satisfied young man with a veneer of breeding and education, and no morals whatever. He was out for a good time at everybody's expense, and the cost to them did not concern him.

The evidence of fact against him was, of course, over-whelming, and there could be no allegation by the defence that identification had been prejudiced by publication of a photograph. Counsel on his behalf put up a strong plea of insanity on the ground that he was a moral defective and therefore should not be held responsible for his actions. Dr Grierson, the experienced medical officer of Brixton Prison, said in the witness box that he had no doubt Heath knew what he was doing and that he was doing wrong. The jury took the same view and with no great delay found a verdict of 'Guilty'. Heath was sentenced to death and executed.

As a postscript to the case, there were questions in the House of Commons about my decision against publication of Heath's photograph, but the Home Secretary had no difficulty in convincing the House that my decision had been the right one in the circumstances.

Chapter 8
THE FINGERPRINT DEPARTMENT

LIKE C.R.O., the Fingerprint Department acts as a central register for the whole of Great Britain and receives from forces all over the country something like 350 records a day covering all serious crimes. It also maintains a regular exchange of prints with Northern Ireland and Eire of those criminals who seem likely to operate on both sides of the Irish Sea. Less frequently, but still fairly often, there are exchanges with the police forces of Western Europe who are members of the International Criminal Police Commission, and occasionally, with the Dominions and other overseas countries. A few years ago, for the first time, a set of fingerprints was transmitted by wireless to Australia and clearly received.

Scotland Yard's Fingerprint Department owes its origin to Sir Edward Henry who, after service as Commissioner of Police in Bengal, joined the Metropolitan Police as Assistant Commissioner in 1901, and was Commissioner from 1903 to 1919. In Bengal he had had experience of the use of fingerprints to distinguish the coolies on the plantations, and it was he who first worked out a system of classification which made it possible to use fingerprints in the identification of criminals. With slight modification, Henry's system is still in use today. It is based on the fact that no two persons have ever been known to possess identical prints. Even those of identical twins are slightly different.

The system depends on the fact that all prints are of one of the following types: loops, arches, whorls or composites. The meaning of these terms is clear from the accompanying illustration.

As all or only one of these forms may occur on the ten fingers of the two hands, their distinction can be made the basis of a system of classification.

To describe the system fully would go beyond the scope of this book, but I have been asked so often to explain how prints are classified that I think it is worth trying to set out as or adding numerators and demoninators:' $\dfrac{31}{31}$

But the total of possible combinations is 32^2 and our fraction formula does not cover the possibility of ten fingers with no whorls at all or $\dfrac{0}{0}$. For convenience we write this as $-$ and add 1 to the final numerator and denominator in all other cases.
Two further examples will make the scheme clear:

$$\dfrac{W}{L} \qquad \dfrac{L}{W} \qquad \dfrac{W}{L} \qquad \dfrac{L}{W} \qquad \dfrac{W}{L}$$

$$\dfrac{16}{0} \qquad \dfrac{0}{8} \qquad \dfrac{4}{0} \qquad \dfrac{0}{2} \qquad \dfrac{1}{0} = \dfrac{21}{10}$$

and, adding 1 top and bottom, $\dfrac{22}{11}$.

simply as possible the main features of the system now in use.

Roughly sixty per cent of all impressions are loops, five per cent arches and thirty-five per cent whorls and composites. For simplicity in the primary classification, arches are included in loops (L) and composites in whorls (W). There are five pairs of fingers and in each pair the prints may be LL WW LW WL. The same possible combinations exist for the second pair, so

on ten fingers.

We have now established 1,024 different groups. Some are found in practice to be small, but others are very large and further subdivision is necessary. The largest group is that in which no whorls are present at all, represented by the formula $\dfrac{1}{1}$. This group is first subdivided by reference to the direction of the ridges of the loops on the index fingers. Some slope towards the ulna, others towards the radius, and are therefore called ulnar loops (U) or radial loops (R). This still leaves a very large sub-group, represented by the formula $\dfrac{1\ U}{1\ U}$, in which both index fingers carry ulnar loops. To subdivide this again, we count the ridges on the index and middle fingers between the outer and inner terminus, as shown in the diagram opposite.

All fingers are fairly evenly divided between those with less (I) and those with more (O) than the average number of such ridges. So on each hand there are four possible combinations: II IO OO OI, or for both hands, sixteen.

Our formula may now read like this:

$$\frac{1}{1} \qquad \frac{U}{U} \qquad \frac{IO}{II}$$

This represents two hands with no whorls on any finger, ulnar loops on the two index fingers, and with more and less ridges than average on the right index and middle fingers respectively, and less than the average on these two fingers on the left hand.

A still further subdivision of these sixteen sub-groups is made by counting the ridges on the little finger of the right hand. So a specimen formula might now read:

$$\frac{1}{1} \qquad \frac{U}{U} \qquad \frac{IO}{II} \qquad 6$$

If a print with this formula is received, the searcher would go to the cabinet containing prints classified $\dfrac{1}{1}$, and in it to the sub-groups $\dfrac{U}{U}$, then to the section $\dfrac{IO}{II}$, and finally would extract for more detailed comparison the comparatively small number of prints with six ridges on the right little finger.

By similar methods still more sub-groups can be established as required, but it would be tiresome to follow them into

INNER TERMINUS   INNER TERMINUS

OUTER TERMINUS   OUTER TERMINUS
(CLOSED DELTA)   (OPEN DELTA)

7 COUNT LOOP   6 COUNT LOOP

In loops all ridges cutting an imaginary line drawn from the outer to
the inner terminus are counted excluding the terminal points.

further detail. The reader who has been sufficiently patient to
follow all this will have grasped the idea.

The main collection of prints is used to link up a criminal
with his previous convictions, so that when he comes before
the court his previous record may be known. From the police
force which has arrested him, or the prison where he has been
lodged, a form is sent to Scotland Yard on which his fingerprints have been impressed. When the form comes in, and the
formula of the prints has been determined, all the cards of that
formula are examined for minor differences, such as breaks in
the ridges, deltas, junctions, loops and so on, corresponding to
those in the new form, with the result that either an identical
set of prints is found or it is clear that no similar print has been
placed on record.

If a print is identified, enlarged photographs of it and of the
recorded print are made and sixteen points of similarity are
marked by arrows. If this number of identical points is found,
the identity of the two prints is presumed to be complete, and
experience in the comparison of thousands of prints over many
years supports the presumption.

On one occasion, some years ago, an examination of the fingerprints of a male offender showed them to be identical with prints filed as those of a woman. The identification was hotly contested and it was suggested that at last the fingerprint system had broken down. But it had not. A 'woman' charged with importuning had 'her' fingerprints taken, was fined forty shillings, and released without any suspicion of 'her' sex being aroused. At the time of her second conviction 'she' had reverted to her true, male, sex.

Sometimes a criminal tries to conceal his identity by sand-papering away the prints on his fingertips, but they soon grow again in the same form. It is even possible to remove the skin from the fingertips of a dead body, after decomposition has begun, and take prints from it. Though the epidermis may have decomposed, the ridges under the skin will have remained and the pattern can be reconstructed from them.

The palm of the hand and the sole of the foot also carry similar distinguishing marks. On one occasion, indeed, Chief Superintendent F. R. Cherrill was able to make an identification from a hand print left at the scene of a crime through a hole in a glove. But the usefulness of such prints is so rare that there would be no point in establishing a collection of them.

The main fingerprint collection at Scotland Yard, consisting of the prints of all ten fingers, includes more than a million and a quarter, and increases at the rate of 50,000 a year. Although the collection is weeded out regularly by removing the prints of people who have died or have reached an age when they are unlikely to indulge in further serious crime, an even more drastic weeding is necessary, and as soon as enough staff is available, all cards relating to offenders who have not come to notice for thirty or even twenty years will be removed. This will involve some risk of missing an occasional case, but in the interests of speed and efficiency that is a risk which must be faced. In any event, the weeded forms are not destroyed but only removed to a 'dead' section.

Weeding is essential, for the time required to make a search depends on the number of prints to be examined, and time is often vitally important, since to be of any practical value a prisoner must be linked with his previous criminal record by the time a case comes into court. Fingerprint work also requires a large and expensive staff and demands great accuracy and concentration. If the collection is allowed to grow too large, the output of each worker will be reduced and the cost of administration will go up.

Besides the main collection, there is also the Single Fingerprint collection, in which prints of the ten fingers are each recorded on a separate card. This collection has an entirely different function from that of the main collection. It is not a question here of linking up a prisoner with his previous history, but of identifying a single print left at the scene of the crime by an unknown person. If all the ten million separate fingerprints in the main collection had to be searched through in making such an identification, the task would be so long and laborious that search would eventually become impracticable. This, indeed, has been the experience of the F.B.I., in America, where the number of prints at one time reached enormous levels.

The single fingerprint collection is therefore limited to the prints of known active offenders, and contains only the prints of the past five years, numbering just over one hundred thousand. Near it is a similar collection for the previous eighteen years, which is only searched in cases of murder or crimes of unusual importance. A special classification based on the form of the central ridges on the index fingertip is adopted for this collection, from which some one hundred and fifty identifications a year are made.

A further collection – the Scenes of Crime collection – includes all unidentified prints left at places where crimes have been committed, and from this collection about 1,750 identifications a year are made. A striking example of the value of this collection occurred some years ago, when the print of a right forefinger, believed to belong to the burglar, was found on a wineglass in a house which had been entered at Watford. A year afterwards, a man was arrested at Hitchin. His prints were taken and sent up to Scotland Yard, and the Fingerprint Department was able to identify the right forefinger with that on the wineglass in their possession. Moreover, during the intervening twelve months, a number of other prints had been found in burgled houses as far afield as Gloucestershire and Leicestershire, filed in the Scenes of Crime Collection, and these, too, were identified as belonging to the same man.

Duplicate papers for a few special groups of people are kept in a separate index. There are frequent inquiries for Indian seamen who have deserted their ships in British ports, and these are filed separately. A sufficient number of people habitually commit sacrilege, justifying a special collection, and there are other 'specialists' such as the I.R.A.

The staff of the Fingerprint Department are all police officers who, as a rule, enter the department fairly early in their service and remain there for many years, if not for the rest of their police career. Their work consists not only in classifying and identifying prints, but in visiting the scenes of crimes to search for any prints left behind, and in giving evidence in court. Here, experience is essential, for if in cross-examination the trustworthiness of fingerprint evidence is called in question, they must be able to assure the court that in years of experience, examining thousands of prints, they have never come across a case in which different persons have possessed identical prints.

In the case of George Russell, accused of murdering an elderly woman recluse at her home in Maidenhead, Chief Superintendent Cherrill was cross-examined at length about a single partial fingerprint found on the lid of a small cardboard box, which the police alleged was that of Russell. There was other evidence against Russell at the trial, but the identification of this fingerprint was essential to the prosecution's case; Cherrill's evidence obviously carried great weight with the jury, and Russell was hanged.

In America and elsewhere, the fingerprint departments are staffed by civilians, and it was decided that the eighty officers employed on this work at Scotland Yard should ultimately be replaced by civilians, in order to release them for other duties. This change will take some years, since it will be essential to retain a number of police officers until the civilian staff has had sufficiently long experience to be able to stand up to examination in court.

Chapter 9
THE FORENSIC SCIENCE LABORATORY

IF he is to be successful, the detective must in many ways cultivate a scientific attitude in his approach to the inquiries that come his way. He must patiently assemble his facts and ignore none, however insignificant. He may form a theory or make an assumption, but he must never be led away by it or attempt to make the facts fit the theory. On the contrary, he must follow the inductive method, drawing his theory from the facts and constantly testing it as new facts emerge.

With this similarity of approach and outlook between the scientist and the detective, it is surprising that only comparatively lately was the scientist called upon to play a regular part in criminal investigation. The pathologist and the toxicologist were an exception. Their views on the causes of death or injury in criminal cases have long been called in evidence, but it is only within the last thirty years that the scientific expert has been recognised by the police as a valuable ally in the investigation of these and less spectacular crimes directed not against the person but against property.

The Forensic Science Laboratory was among the many innovations which Scotland Yard owes to Lord Trenchard, who established it at Hendon in 1934, to serve not only the Metropolitan Police, but also the police forces of the Home Counties.

Naturally it took time for detective officers to realise fully the ways in which the Laboratory could help them, and feeling it was important to establish close contact between the C.I.D. and the Laboratory, I took an early opportunity of moving it to Scotland Yard, where it was more easily accessible. I encouraged officers of all ranks to visit the Laboratory to learn about its possibilities, and direct instruction on the subject is given in the course at the Detective Training School. As the resources of the Laboratory have become more widely known, the calls upon it have steadily increased.

For the most part, examination of the material submitted

calls for the services of the chemist or the biologist, but the physicist and the mineralogist are also needed from time to time. When the staff of the Laboratory does not possess the necessary experience, outside experts are called in. In particular, the Laboratory relies on outside help in the field of pathology. The police in London have been able to call upon the services of a long line of distinguished pathologists, including Dr Keith Simpson and Dr Donald Teare and the late Sir Bernard Spilsbury.

In cases involving the use of explosives the Laboratory can enlist the help of the Home Office Chief Inspector of Explosives, and for many years Mr Robert Churchill has examined firearms or ammunition used in crimes.

The chemist plays perhaps the most important part in the work of the Laboratory. A knowledge of poisons and drugs, whether organic or inorganic, of dyes, paints and colours, of explosives and inflammable materials, of medicines, metals and glass, will all, at one time or another, be essential, as will many techniques which, strictly speaking, lie within the domain of the physicist, such as spectroscopic analysis or the use of ultra-violet and infra-red rays.

The biologist must be able to identify all sorts of materials, animal or vegetable, such as seeds, splinters of wood or saw-dust, blood and semen, or human and animal hairs, and to distinguish fibres of any kind, animal, vegetable, mineral or synthetic. He must be an œcologist and know the characteristic flora and fauna of different types of country, the seasons at which plants flower or seed, and their methods of seed dispersal. His knowledge must extend to the mosses, fungi and algae, and to microscopic forms of animal and plant life. With the aid of the mineralogist, he will need to recognise the different types of soil according to their mineral content.

One of the most important forms of study in which chemist, biologist and mineralogist must co-operate is that of dusts, for these often can be used to link up a criminal with the scene of his crime. Dusts are of infinite variety and may contain animal or plant substances or mineral matter, derived either directly from the earth or living things, or from manufactured materials. They are divided into four main types: road dust, airborne dust, industrial dust found around such places as cement works, flour mills or paint factories; and occupational dust, such as the soot or coal dust on the sweep or the miner, or the yeast and moulds found on the clothing of workers in a brewery.

All these things the scientist can usually identify, but it is the special task of the forensic scientist to interpret them and show how they may be of use as evidence. They will not always suffice of themselves to establish a case, but they may serve to corroborate or disprove statements made by witnesses, to clear up an uncertainty, fill a gap in evidence or strengthen a conclusion.

The wide scope of the Laboratory can be illustrated by four cases, each of which shows how one or other of the branches does its work.

First the biological branch. In a top-floor flat in South-East London were two families. The first consisted of a man, his wife and two daughters; the second, of his married daughter, her husband and their baby. Relations between the families were at times strained, and one day the son-in-law made a vicious attack on his father-in-law. One evening about a week later, most of the household were out, only the mother-in-law and her son-in-law being at home. One of the daughters returned at about eleven o'clock and found her mother lying dead in a pool of blood. She had been attacked with a knife while lying on her bed, and had no fewer than twenty-four stab wounds. From their position it was clear that she had fought desperately for her life and that her attacker was likely to have a quantity of blood upon his clothes.

On a blanket in the son-in-law's room was the bloodstained shape of a left handprint, and on the door of the room was a smear of blood. A search was made for the weapon, but nothing was discovered, nor could the son-in-law be found.

About three days later, at three in the morning, a policeman at Ramsgate stopped a man, who was wearing only a raincoat, a shirt, a pair of shoes, a wrist-watch and a ring. His story was that he had been swimming and that his clothes had been stolen. It sounded unlikely to the policeman who suspected him at once of being the missing son-in-law, his description having been circulated. Eventually the man admitted that he was, but he emphatically denied that he knew anything about the murder.

His few remaining clothes and other belongings were examined at the Laboratory. On the mackintosh were stains of human blood. There were smears of it inside the backs of the shoes where the fingers would normally go to ease them into position. The ring also gave a positive reaction for blood, and though none was obvious on the wrist-watch, when the back was unscrewed, a thin crust of blood was exposed showing that some had percolated between the metal faces.

Most of the blood was found to belong to the dead woman's blood group, and so were the stains left on the blanket and the bedroom door. The rest of the evidence against the son-in-law amounted to no more than suspicion. Only the Laboratory's evidence was firm, and on this he was charged with murder. At his trial it was pointed out that it was unfortunate he had lost his clothes because, if he were innocent and they could have been produced, they might have been found free of blood. On the other hand, if they were bloodstained it was obviously of the highest importance to him that they should not be found. The jury brought in a verdict of guilty.

A case with which the physics branch had to deal began when two men were stopped in a car on suspicion that they had broken into a shop and stolen some goods. Both men emphatically denied this. Nevertheless, their clothing, together with sweepings from the floor of the car and pieces of glass from the broken door of the shop, were taken to the Laboratory for examination. From the sweepings taken from the car, the Laboratory picked out some small pieces of glass. Other small fragments were found in the men's clothing, and both were compared with the glass from the broken window. At the trial a scientific expert from the Laboratory gave evidence that all the glass had similar physical characteristics, which indicated a common origin. Both prisoners tried to meet this evidence, one by saying that the glass on his clothing was from a tumbler broken in a public house, the other by explaining that glass had got on his clothing from a broken window in his home. Pieces of the tumbler, and of the broken window, were therefore obtained and compared with the fragments recovered from the men's clothing and sweepings from the car, but they were found to be entirely different. As the judge pointed out to the jury, the evidence of the expert seemed irrefutable and showed that both prisoners must have been at the shop at or about the time the glass was broken. Eventually both men were convicted.

The chemical branch is often called upon in 'hit and run' motoring cases. One winter evening the police were called to a road in Sutton, Surrey, where a cyclist had been seriously injured. A young woman walking along a dimly-lit section of the road had seen a lorry hit the cyclist, who was pushing his machine up a slight hill on the opposite side of the road. The lorry gave a lurch and drove on at a fast speed. The girl called an ambulance and the police, and the man was taken to hospital, but a few days later he died without having been able to speak. The witness, as often happens in such cases, could give no more information than that the lorry was an open one – didn't see the index number. A B.B.C. broadcast produced one other witness, a man who had been nearby and had seen a lorry drive past him very fast. He had heard a bump, and a minute afterwards had come upon the injured man and the young woman. He had not seen the number of the lorry, but about three-quarters of an hour later, when he was still at the spot, he saw a similar lorry drive past in the opposite direction, and had noticed that the index letters were FLX, though he had not seen the number.

With this slender information, the police had the Motor Registration records examined for all lorries of a similar type with the index letters FLX. One by one many lorries were traced and examined, their owners and drivers questioned, and their stories checked. There were many disappointments, but at last a lorry was found which had had one of its headlamps recently torn off. There was also some slight damage, which seemed to be fresh, on the front near side. The lorry was one of several owned by a Surrey firm, and it could have been driven by one of several men working late. They were all questioned, but each denied having had the lorry out at the time concerned. No satisfactory explanation could be got for the damage, but in the absence of other evidence police inquiries seemed to have reached a deadlock.

At this stage it was decided to ask for the Laboratory's assistance. Examination of the bicycle and clothing of the dead man showed that the bicycle had been hit by the bumper of the lorry, for an imprint of the bumper could be seen in the dents caused by the impact, and small flakes of paint that did not belong to the cycle were sticking to the damaged parts of it. Further evidence was found on the dead man's coat and trousers, where black and green marks – probably paint – were discovered in the fibres on the shoulder and back.

These exhibits were preserved for detailed examination in

the Laboratory, and the damaged lorry was then examined in its garage. A slight dent was found in the bumper and, more significantly, the paint, of which there was a number of coats, was missing over an area comparable with the amount of paint found on the bicycle. Samples of all the paints on the lorry – black and green – were removed, and the exhibits taken to the Laboratory. There, detailed examination and analysis proved unmistakably that the paints and marks on the bicycle and clothing were identical with, and must have come from, the suspected lorry. Confronted with these facts, one of the factory staff admitted having driven the lorry on the night in question on the road where the accident had happened. He was duly charged and convicted.

A somewhat odd example of the work of the Laboratory shows how unexpected are the by-ways into which the detective may be led by his inquiries. Towards the end of 1952, the bookmakers in a certain London district came to the police and alleged that they were being defrauded by a gang who were forging betting slips in order to claim winnings on bets which had never been made. The slips were given to the bookmaker in the usual way, with the names of the selected horses and the stakes written on them in pencil. The punters had asked to have the slips back after the race, as they wished to keep a record of their bets, and to this the bookmaker agreed. At the end of the day he handed the slips back after cancelling them by drawing diagonal lines with a ball-point pen across the pencilled entries.

It was this arrangement that gave the fraudulent punters their chance. They took the cancelled slips away, rubbed out the pencilled names, and substituted, in the ink used by the bookmaker, the name or names of certain of the winning horses. They then returned to the bookmaker and claimed that the slip had been cancelled in error, whereas in fact some of the horses named on it had won their races. Though he could not understand how a mistake could have occurred, the bookmaker paid up. But when the manoeuvre was repeated by a number of people, he became suspicious. Eventually, when a sum of fifty pounds was demanded on a double, he called in the police.

Detectives took a number of the suspected slips to the Laboratory for examination. Under the microscope, particles of graphite from the original pencilled entries could plainly be seen, and examination under the infra-red rays revealed parts of the original pencil letters and figures. Further scrutiny of the places where the horses' names written in ink crossed over, instead of under, the cancellation strokes, showed that names had been written after the strokes were made. On this evidence three men were charged and convicted of conspiracy, false pretences and uttering forged documents, and were sentenced to various terms of imprisonment.

The aim of the Laboratory is to provide an impartial record of findings and the reasonable inferences to be drawn from them. They may be for or against an accused person. Many cases never come to court, because the Laboratory findings are strongly in favour of the innocence of an accused man. Sometimes, indeed, the services of the Laboratory are used by the defence, as in the Christie case, where the defence asked for the exhumation of Mrs Beryl Evans, and the Laboratory examination was conducted as much on their behalf as on behalf of the prosecution.

In another case a man charged with receiving a stolen cycle had been committed for trial. The defence protested his innocence and asked for the cycle to be examined at the Laboratory. There, it was found to be of a different make from the machine that had been stolen, it had never been painted in the manner suggested by the prosecution, nor were the mudguards made of the material which the prosecution had named. In those circumstances, the prosecution offered no evidence, and the man was discharged.

A more dramatic case was that in which a man was alleged to have strangled his wife. He had been found by the police with his head in a gas oven, but the effects of gas poisoning, if there had ever been any, had worn off. Mr L. C. Nickolls, the head of the Laboratory, had given evidence for the prosecution and was sitting in court when the defence put forward its story. It was that during a quarrel, the accused man had got his wife by the throat and she had suddenly gone limp. He found that she was dead, and in his remorse he had tried to commit suicide and must have lain for nearly forty-eight hours unconscious on the floor.

Mr Nickolls immediately volunteered some information to the defence. It had been found that the defendant had urinated in his clothing, and that the urine had abstracted dye from the carpet in front of the gas oven. The dye had percolated the

99

man's clothing and stained his underclothes. This staining could only have happened after very long contact between the carpet and the wet garments. Thus at least one part of the man's story was confirmed. The defence, on hearing of this, asked for Mr Nickolls to be recalled, and in the light of his new evidence the jury brought in a verdict of manslaughter.

Perhaps the Laboratory's greatest triumph during my Commissionership was a case in which no charge was ever brought. One day in May, 1948, a local resident walking on the golf course at Potters Bar saw a human hand and arm lying in a pond. He informed the police, who dragged and drained the pond and in the next few days found the remaining parts of a human body which had been totally dismembered. When the parts were assembled, the body proved to be that of a man of about five feet six inches in height, and about thirty-five to forty-five years old. There was a hole in the front of the skull and inside were two pieces of bone which indicated that death had been caused by a violent blow on the forehead. The parts were in an advanced stage of decomposition, and Dr Teare reported that in his opinion death had occurred four to eight months before. An immediate check was made of all men who had been reported missing during that time, and they were all accounted for except one, Albert William Welch, aged forty-five, who had disappeared from his home in Potters Bar on November 17, 1947. Inquiries pointed to the probability that the remains were those of Welch, but it was the work of the Laboratory that eventually satisfied the coroner's jury of their identity.

The Laboratory concentrated on three main items. First, the skull. A photograph of Welch was obtained, and transparent copies of it and of a photograph of the skull found in the pond were superimposed on one another. The outlines and main features showed so close a resemblance that there was no doubt the skull could have been that of Welch. Second, the teeth. It was known that all Welch's teeth had been extracted some years before. So had those of the skull. There was some indication of an abcess on the upper jaw, and Welch was known to have complained of pain there some time before his disappearance. Finally, the feet. The police obtained from Welch's wife a pair of his boots, and a cast in plaster of Paris and gelatine was made of the inside of each boot. To avoid the risk of shrinkage, the casts were photographed immediately.

The photographs showed the imprint of feet in the boots, and in particular the mark of a slightly enlarged big toe. X-ray photographs were taken of the feet from the pond, after one of them, which had become disarticulated through decomposition, had been carefully reassembled. Transparent photos of the X-ray pictures were then superimposed on the photographs of the internal casts of the boots, and Dr Holden, then head of the Laboratory, told the coroner's jury that in his view there was a remarkably accurate fit between the X-ray photographs and the impressions in the boots.

I took considerable interest in this remarkable work of reconstruction by the Laboratory, but the staff, like any other group of scientists, was intent on a technical job, and to them the question of murder was a secondary matter. They had the remains of a body. Whose was it?

What the Laboratory did get was sufficient evidence to establish the identity of Welch to the satisfaction of a coroner's jury, for which they were congratulated by the coroner. The jury found a verdict of wilful murder by a person or persons unknown, and named the date of death as November 17 or 18, 1947. Not even the Laboratory, however, could help the police to bring the crime home to anyone.

Chapter 10
CHRISTIE

THE case of John Reginald Halliday Christie aroused special interest not only because it involved a series of murders extending over ten years, but because of the problem created by Christie's confession to a murder for which another man had already been convicted and executed. Coincidence has a notoriously long arm, but to many people it seemed incredible that a series of murders could be committed in the same house by two different men.

The story begins in March, 1953, in that grim house at 10 Rillington Place, Notting Hill, where Christie and his wife had rented the ground floor flat since 1938. One day towards the end of March, another tenant, who had arranged to use the kitchen on the ground floor, went there to fix some brackets for a wireless set. Noticing when he tapped the wall that it sounded hollow, he tore off some of the wallpaper and shone a torch through the opening. Inside he saw the bare back of a human body. He called the police, and they found that behind the wallpaper the door of a coal cupboard had been nailed up. In the cupboard were the bodies of three women. The police also noticed that in the front room some of the floorboards were loose, and on taking them up, they found underneath the body of a fourth woman, covered with earth.

During the next few days the police ransacked the house from floor to roof, removing floors and fireplaces and pulling down hollow walls, but with no further result. They dug up the back garden, however, and there found a number of human bones. Examination of the bodies found in the house showed that all four women had died from asphyxia, and in three cases there was evidence of strangulation and carbon monoxide poisoning.

The body under the floorboards was identified by her brother and sister from Sheffield as that of Mrs Christie. The last news the sister had had from her was in a letter dated December 15, 1952, to which Christie had added a note saying,

'Ethel has no envelopes so I posted this for her at work.' At Christmas, the sister had received a letter from Christie, saying his wife had asked him to write the Christmas cards as she had rheumatism in her fingers. On January 17 the sister wrote to Mrs Christie, but received no reply.

None of the neighbours had seen Mrs Christie since just before Christmas, and Christie himself had told various people a series of conflicting stories. To some, he had said that he and his wife had quarrelled and she had gone away; to others, that he was going to a new job which he described at one time as being in Birmingham and at others in Northampton, Chester or Sheffield. His wife, according to these stories, had preceded him.

Suspicion inevitably fell upon Christie, for he had left the house without notice on March 19, after letting it to new tenants, though, in fact, he had no right to let it at all. He borrowed a suitcase from them, and they saw him pack into it various articles of women's clothing. Suspicion against him was strengthened when examination of the letter of December 15 showed the date to have been altered, and when the other tenants in the house recalled that from time to time since October, 1952, they had seen Christie pour disinfectant down the drains and sprinkle it on the passage floor.

The police sought for Christie in likely places all over London, and in their search they naturally visited the common lodging houses in which wanted criminals often seek anonymity. As a result Christie was fairly quickly traced to Rowton House in King's Cross Road, where he had stayed from March 20 to 25. He had left, however, before the police arrived.

On that day the newspapers carried long stories about the murders, and early in the morning a police constable on duty at Putney Embankment saw a man leaning over the river wall. He challenged the man, who gave the name of Waddington, an example of how criminals often lack imagination, for this, though the constable did not know it at the time, was the name of Christie's brother-in-law. The constable was not satisfied and asked the man to go along with him to Putney Police Station. A police van happened to pass at that moment, and they got in. On the way, without saying anything, the man took out an identity card and flicked it across to the constable. It bore the name of John Christie.

At the police station Christie was interviewed by a Chief

Inspector, who told him of the finding of the body of Mrs Christie and asked if he wished to say anything about it. Christie, an insignificant, bald man with thick-lensed glasses who looked more like a harassed clerk than a murderer, immediately began to cry.

'She woke me up, and was choking,' he said. 'I couldn't stand it any longer . . . You know what I did.'

At this the Chief Inspector thought it right to caution him, and Christie then made a statement. In it he said he had woken up on the night of December 14 to find his wife convulsive, blue in the face, and choking. He had taken a stocking and tied it round her neck to put her to sleep. Then he went on, 'I left her in bed two or three days and didn't know what to do. Then I remembered some loose floorboards in the front room and I believe I went back and put her in a blanket and half dragged, half carried her down and put her in and covered her with earth.'

He went on to describe the sale of his furniture after Christmas, and of his wife's wedding ring and gold watch, which he sold to a jeweller in Shepherd's Bush because he was hard up. This part of his story was quickly verified by reference to the jeweller, who produced his buying book with Christie's correct signature and address.

When arrested, Christie had on him a receipt for a registered letter addressed to the Yorkshire Penny Bank in Sheffield. This branch had received a letter dated January 26, 1953, signed Ethel Christie, closing the account and asking for the balance. The bank sent a sum of ten pounds, fifteen shillings and twopence, and received as receipt a cheque signed 'Ethel Christie'. The signatures on the letter and the cheque were very good imitations of the dead woman's signature, and did not attract any suspicion at the bank. On this evidence Christie was charged with the murder of his wife, brought before the magistrate, and remanded in custody so that the police could complete their inquiries.

In his statement Christie had spoken of chronic headaches, giddiness, fibrositis and acute diarrhoea, for which he had received medical treatment at various times from 1948 to 1952. His doctor confirmed this, and said that in July, 1952, Christie had been advised to enter a mental hospital as a voluntary patient, but had declined to do so.

The police continued to make inquiries into the identity of

the three bodies found in the cupboard, and it was not long before they were identified by relations or friends, while various people were found who had last seen the different women with a man whom they identified as Christie. He himself gave an account of how he had met these three women casually, and how they had gone with him to his flat. In each case, according to Christie, an argument had developed, the women had refused to leave, and there had been some sort of a struggle, resulting in the women falling down on the ground or on to a chair. Christie professed not to be able to remember exactly what had happened. In one case he thought the woman's clothing must have got caught round her neck; in another, he found the woman lying in a chair with a rope round her neck; in the third, she was just on the floor. He supposed that each time he must have put the body in the cupboard.

The post-mortem examination, however, showed that in each body, except that of Mrs Christie, there was evidence of carbon monoxide poisoning – an important point in view of Christie's own statement later about the way in which he had dealt with one of the two women whose skeletons were found in the garden.

A team of police officers dug over the whole garden two feet deep, down to the clay, which had not been disturbed. The work lasted several days, and as a result a number of human bones, hair, clothes and pieces of newspaper were recovered. The bones were taken to the Anatomy Department at London Hospital, and there sorted out and assembled into two almost complete skeletons, from which only a skull and a few bones were missing. Although one skull had disintegrated, it was reconstructed from ninety-two broken pieces of bone. It was, however, uncertain to which body this remarkable reconstruction belonged. To make sure that no small pieces had been missed, all the soil in the garden was carefully sieved, and this resulted in the discovery of some teeth and a fourth cervical vertebra. On this additional evidence, the anatomists were able to allocate this skull with certainty to one of the bodies.

Inquiry for the missing skull was made of all nearby police stations and of the local coroner, and the records showed that when the police were investigating the murder of a Mrs Evans at the same address in 1949, they had learned that Christie's dog had dug up a skull in the garden and that Christie had thrown it into the basement of a bombed house, where it had been found by the police in 1949. Examination by the pathologist at that time had shown the skull to be that of a woman about thirty-three years of age. The matter was reported to the coroner, but as there was no evidence as to the history of the skull, it was thought to be probably that of someone killed during the blitz. Now, of course, there was little doubt that it belonged to the second skeleton assembled from the remains found in Christie's garden.

The flesh of both bodies had entirely gone, and examination of the soil suggested that both had been buried, fully clothed, some nine or ten years before, and had decomposed where the bones were found. From these remains, the anatomists were able to say that the skeletons were those of two women. One, whose skull had been reconstructed, was about twenty-one years of age, about five feet seven or eight in height, and had had one of her teeth crowned with a palladium silver alloy in the manner characteristic of Central European dentistry. The second woman was from thirty to thirty-four years of age and about five feet one or two inches in height.

The cases of these two women occupied a relatively minor place at Christie's trial, so that no great public attention was paid to the remarkable feat of reconstruction by the anatomists of London Hospital. A reference to the registry of Missing Persons at Scotland Yard, however, supplied confirmation of all they had done. The registry showed that in August, 1943, a young refugee from Vienna had disappeared. Her name was Ruth Fuerst, and she was then aged twenty-one. In the garden the police had found fragments of a burned newspaper dated May 9, 1943. Another missing person was a woman, Muriel Amelia Eady, aged thirty-two, who worked at a radio factory in Park Royal. She had left her aunt's home in Putney on October 9, 1944, saying, 'I shan't be late,' and was never seen again. She was then wearing a black frock, and the remains of a black silk dress were found in Christie's garden.

The police were reasonably sure that these were the women whose bones had been found in the garden, but after so long an interval they could find no evidence of any association between them and Christie. On June 5, therefore, by agreement with Christie's solicitors, the Chief Inspector in charge of the case went to see him in Brixton Prison where he was awaiting trial. The Inspector asked him if he wished to say anything

106

about the remains found in the garden, whereupon Christie made a statement which confirmed the identity of the two women. He said he had met Fuerst in 1943, and that she had gone to his flat where he strangled her with a rope and buried her in the garden. Some months later, while digging there, he had unearthed a skull and put it in the dustbin which he used as an incinerator.

Later, when he was working at a radio factory, he had met Muriel Eady. He described how, on a visit to his flat, she had complained of catarrh and he had induced her to inhale some Friar's Balsam through a tube attached to a jar. He connected the inlet tube to a gas point, but the balsam disguised the smell of the gas and the girl became unconscious. It will be remembered that three of the bodies found in the house contained traces of carbon monoxide poisoning. Christie added that he had a vague recollection of tying a stocking round the woman's neck and later burying her in the garden, fully clothed. In a later statement he said he could not remember if it was Ruth Fuerst or Muriel Eady whom he had gassed, and he gave an account of the disposal of the skull, which was Muriel Eady's, on the bombed site in 1949.

In this statement, which was made to the police in the presence of his solicitor, Christie for the first time referred to events leading up to the death of Mrs Evans in 1949. The brief facts of this case were that on December 2, 1949, the bodies of Mrs Evans and her fourteen-months-old daughter, Geraldine, had been found hidden in a wash-house in the backyard at 10 Rillington Place. Death in both cases was due to strangulation. Evans, who occupied rooms above Christie, had left Rillington Place on November 14, and was later found at Merthyr Tydfil and brought back to London, where he confessed to having strangled his wife and child. On January 13, 1950, he was charged at the Central Criminal Court with these murders. The prosecution decided to proceed with the charge of murdering the child, though most of the evidence concerning the wife came out. Christie and his wife both gave evidence for the prosecution, and it was put to Christie in cross-examination that he was responsible for both deaths, or at least knew much more about them than he had said. His answer was, 'That is a lie.' Although at the trial Evans withdrew the confession made in his statement to the police, the jury did not believe his denial and found him guilty of the murder of the child. He was later executed.

Christie now said in his statement to the police that on two successive days in November, 1949, he had gone upstairs to see Mrs Evans. On the first occasion he found she had attempted to gas herself, but he opened the door and windows and she came round. The next day he went up again and, according to his story, she asked him to help her to commit suicide. He turned on the gas and held the pipe near her face. When she became unconscious he turned the tap off. He went on, 'I think that's when I strangled her. I think it was with a stocking I found in the room.' When he saw Evans, he told him his wife had gassed herself, but that no doubt he, Evans, would be suspected of having killed her because of the rows and fights he had had with his wife. Evans seemed to think the same, and said he would take the body of his wife away in his van and leave it somewhere.

At Christie's trial, which began on June 22, 1953, the prosecution chose to proceed with the charge of murdering his wife. The defence did not suggest he had not murdered her, but sought to obtain a verdict of 'Guilty but insane'. To establish this, questions were asked not only about the death of Mrs Christie, but also about the deaths of the five women whose remains were found in the house and garden, and of Mrs Evans. It was a somewhat curious position, with the defence seeking to lay as many murders at Christie's door as possible, and the prosecution concentrating upon one only.

When asked why he now gave a different account of Mrs Evans' death from the one he had given at Evans' trial, Christie said he had then lied about it 'because I had been accused of killing both of them . . . I think it was because I never interfered with or touched the baby.'

He said that the facts about Mrs Evans had gone right out of his mind when he was arrested on March 31, but he had since seen his solicitor, as well as doctors on both sides, and now he remembered much more than he had been able to remember then.

It was noticeable that, while he was hazy about the details of the other murders he claimed to have committed, saying frequently, 'I don't remember' or 'I suppose I must have done', in the case of Mrs Evans and her baby he was absolutely definite about what had occurred.

The jury were then confronted by that conflict of medical

evidence which makes me more than ever convinced that the simplicity of the M'Naghten Rules is the only practical way for a non-technical jury to define insanity. For the defence, a psychologist argued that Christie was insane. For the prosecution, another psychologist and Dr Mattheson, the experienced medical officer of Brixton Prison, said that he was legally sane.

Summing up, Mr Justice Finnemore reminded the jury that although they had heard much about the deaths of six other women and the Evans baby, there had been no cross-examination of Christie on his statements about them, and they were concerned only with the death of Mrs Christie and with Christie's state of mind at the time. As to that, it had been argued that this succession of murders was evidence of abnormality; but the question was, not whether Christie was abnormal but whether in the terms of the M'Naghten Rules he knew what he was doing, and if he did, whether he knew it was wrong. The jury spent an hour and twenty-two minutes considering their verdict, and found him guilty.

So far as Christie was concerned, that was the end of the matter, but his evidence about Mrs Evans was felt by many people to throw doubt on the result of the trial of Evans three years before. It is true that Evans was executed for the murder of his daughter, not his wife, but if there was any truth in Christie's new story, it might be that he had murdered the child as well as Mrs Evans. The possibility of a miscarriage of justice in a capital case, though remote, is not a matter that can be left in doubt, and the Home Secretary therefore decided that a full inquiry must be made into the circumstances of the deaths of Mrs Evans and her child. Mr John Scott-Henderson, Q.C., was appointed to conduct the inquiry, and to assist him the Home Secretary decided to appoint an experienced police officer. So that there might be no suggestion of prejudice, the officer chosen was the Assistant Chief Constable of the West Riding, who had previously had nothing at all to do with either case.

Mr Scott-Henderson reviewed all the relevant evidence in each trial, all the police reports, the depositions before the magistrates, the briefs and other documents prepared by the solicitors for the defence in each case, and heard evidence from everyone who, it was suggested, might be able to help. In all, he saw twenty-three people, in addition to Christie himself. Christie was at that time a condemned man awaiting execution, and his replies to Mr Scott-Henderson were very different from the evidence he had given at his own trial.

In effect, he was not prepared to say one way or the other whether he was responsible for the death of Mrs Evans. In the course of his remarks he said, 'It is still fogged, and if someone said, "Well, it is obvious you did and there is enough proof about it," then I accept that I did.' Finally, in a conversation with the chaplain at Pentonville Prison, Christie said that in the course of his interviews with his solicitor he became confused and gained the impression that it was necessary for him to confess to murders, 'the more the merrier'.

Mr Scott-Henderson's definite conclusion was that the case against Evans for the murder of his daughter was overwhelming, and that there could be no doubt that he was responsible for that of his wife, too. He also gave it as his opinion that Christie had gradually concluded it would be helpful to his defence if he confessed to the murder of Mrs Evans, but that his statements on this subject were not only unreliable but untrue.

On July 13, Mr Scott-Henderson made his reports to the Home Secretary, just a week after the inquiry began, and on July 15, Christie was executed at Pentonville. So ended a remarkable case in which the work of the detective officers concerned was completed by that of the pathologist and the Forensic Science Laboratory. If, for a short time, it seemed to indicate a possible miscarriage of justice in the case of Evans, this was cleared up by the searching inquiry conducted by Mr Scott-Henderson. It is still safe to say that the risk of an innocent man being executed is so remote that it can be disregarded.

Chapter 11
THE FLYING SQUAD

THE popular conception of the Flying Squad seems to be that of a body of police officers in high-powered cars who are regularly engaged in exciting chases at seventy miles an hour through the streets of London. They can and do engage in such escapades when the need arises, but their day-to-day work is less spectacular. They owe their name, not to the speed of their cars, but to the fact that, unlike the divisional detectives, they are not limited to a particular area but have a roving commission extending over the entire Metropolitan Police District.

Although most crime is local in character, many serious crimes of house-breaking and robbery are committed by criminals who, working singly or in gangs, range over a wide field. In the last thirty years, improved means of transport, and especially the motor car, have greatly increased the opportunities of this type of criminal, and he does not tidily confine his crimes within divisional boundaries. To counter his activities it was necessary to set up a body of picked detectives who were equally free to go wherever their inquiry might lead. The Flying Squad was started in 1919, with about twelve men. Its numbers were gradually increased until, at the end of the war, there were between forty and fifty officers under a Chief Inspector. Faced by the great increase in crime in post-war years, I decided that the importance of the Squad warranted the promotion of the officer in charge to Chief Superintendent and an increase in numbers up to about eighty.

It is the business of Flying Squad officers to make themselves acquainted with all the more dangerous criminals of the Metropolis, and to develop contacts with all sorts of people who may be able to give them information about crimes already committed, or which are being planned. They necessarily become known after a time, because of their activities and their frequent appearances in court. For this reason there are fairly frequent changes in the Squad, for if an officer becomes too well known to the criminal world, his usefulness is greatly impaired.

111

Before the creation of the Flying Squad, this difficulty was met by employing a small group of officers exclusively on the collection of information. It was understood that they themselves would not undertake any inquiries, but would pass on their information to other officers for action so that they themselves should remain unknown and unrecognised. The Ghost Squad, as the newspapers christened it, was incorporated in the original Flying Squad, and a little group of officers continues to act in this way.

Whenever I went out with the Flying Squad, as I did several times, the evening was usually uneventful. On one occasion we drove up to the West End, cruised around the back streets of Soho, stopped, and had a walk along Coventry Street, where the officers pointed out for my edification one or two old clients. Then we drove towards Knightsbridge, circled round one or two likely mews, and our hopes were raised by a wireless message that a stolen car was being driven up from Hammersmith in our direction. To hear a car chase on the radio is rather like listening-in to a running commentary of a football match in which one's sympathies are engaged. Two or three messages followed each other: the stolen car was getting near to us; no, someone else was heading it off; and finally and irrevocably, another police car had anticipated us by stopping it somewhere down in Chelsea.

So we returned towards the West End, drove through Covent Garden and the Strand, and paid another visit to Soho. Here there was a little rowdyism, which the officers quickly stopped with a paternal 'Move along, there, please'. In Poland Street a burglar alarm was ringing furiously, but that, too, was a false alarm, and we asked the local police station to take care of it. That was the sum total of our two-hour patrol. That, unless the underworld had been warned to be on its best behaviour for the Commissioner, is a fair sample of the Flying Squad's routine. But one can judge that it is not always so peaceful from the reports which the Squad renders every three months. It is a poor quarterly period that does not show some two hundred arrests and the recovery of nearly £4,000 worth of stolen goods.

It is regarded as a great distinction to be selected for the Squad, for its members work very much on their own, organising their business as they think best, and operating over a wider field than does the ordinary detective. The Squad has

112

thirty-two cars, each equipped with two-way wireless, so that constant contact can be maintained with Scotland Yard and with other cars. Except when they are engaged in an inquiry, the cars are continually on the move, gathering information and watching for signs of criminal activity.

There are often considerable risks to be run in Flying Squad work. Early in 1949 the Squad was looking for a man named Arthur Parkyn, who was wanted for inflicting grievous bodily harm on a police officer. 'Information received' led the Squad to believe that he was in possession of a stolen Bedford van and had arranged to pick up some property near Clapham Common on January 18. A watch was kept by officers in a 'Q' car – a nondescript van – and as soon as Parkyn and his companion drove up, a wireless message was sent to three Flying Squad cars waiting some distance away.

When the Bedford van moved off, it was followed by the 'Q' car, which kept the Squad cars informed of the direction in which Parkyn was going. By skilful driving the police cars managed to overtake him in Sloane Street. He was driving very fast and they called on him to stop, but as he took no notice, the driver of one Squad car forced him into the kerb and brought him to a halt, while the other two police cars drew up alongside and the officers surrounded the stolen van. Parkyn and his companion struck out at them with a jemmy and a hammer, then Parkyn drove forward suddenly, knocking the officers off the running-board as he collided with the police car, and proceeded to drive his van violently backwards and forwards in a deliberate attempt to crush the Flying Squad men against the other cars. Finally he turned sharply on to the pavement, and, regardless of the pedestrians, drove along it for twenty yards, and so escaped towards Chelsea. One police car managed to follow him, and saw him twice mount the pavement to escape heavy traffic, causing more people to leap out of his way. Eventually the police lost sight of the van, which was later found abandoned on the Albert Embankment.

The next thing the police heard was that two men answering the description of the thieves had boarded a 49 bus going to the Crystal Palace. A wireless message was sent out, and was received by officers in a wireless car patrolling in Streatham High Road. They had just seen a 49 bus pass, and on inquiring of the conductor, learned that two men had just left it and boarded a number 133 bus. They caught up with this, and found Parkyn and his companion, Berlinski, sitting on the top deck. Both denied their identity, and said they were going to South Croydon to look for work, but the officers were not satisfied and took them to their car, intending to bring them in to Gipsy Hill police station. On the way they were met by one of the Flying Squad cars, the officers in which at once identified the prisoners. Outside the police station, Parkyn made a last desperate attempt to escape, but was overpowered. Both men had on them large bunches of ignition keys capable of unlocking almost any vehicle on the road.

In due course they appeared before the Lord Chief Justice, and were convicted of attempted murder and receiving. Parkyn was sentenced to twelve years' penal servitude and Berlinski to seven years. After pronouncing sentence, Lord Goddard asked Inspector Bradford of the Flying Squad to stand up, and said, 'Inspector, I think you and the other members of the Flying Squad are much to be commended for your action in this case. All of you showed considerable courage, and the community are much indebted to you for bringing to justice two dangerous criminals. They way in which you managed to effect the arrest within such a short time in an entirely different part of London shows what a high state of efficiency the Police Force has come to in this country, and in London especially. The thanks of the community are due to you.'

For cold-blooded courage, there are few examples to equal that of Sergeant Deans of the Flying Squad, who received the King's Police Medal for Gallantry, now the George Medal, for his exploit. In 1947, information was received that a gang of thieves proposed to waylay an official of the Kentish Town branch of the Midland Bank, steal his keys and rob the bank. It was learned that for some time members of the gang had been watching and following the bank official, so as to get to know his habits and movements when he left the bank to return home. It was known that the place where he would be waylaid had been decided upon and a plan made for his disposal after the bank had been robbed.

Deans, who was similar in build and appearance to the bank official, volunteered to impersonate him on the evening arranged for the hold-up. It was a bitterly cold night and there was snow on the ground. Knowing that he was being followed, Deans walked calmly down the footpath from the station near the bank official's home. Two men hurried past him, while a third remained behind. He heard a voice say 'Right', then felt a stunning blow on his head, which flung him to the ground. As he lay there he was kicked and beaten, and then flung into a motor van. A scarf was tied over his eyes, adhesive plaster fixed across his mouth, and his hands and ankles were tied together. Then the keys of the bank were taken from him, the van stopped, and he was thrown out face downwards on to a pile of snow.

He managed to free himself and staggered to a house about fifty yards away, where he was taken in and attended to. When the Divisional Police Surgeon arrived, Deans was found to be suffering from concussion and exposure to the severe cold. He was subsequently off duty for two months. Later, at the scene of the assault, a woollen stocking was found loaded with three and a half pounds of wet sand.

While he had been acting as the decoy, other officers of the Flying Squad had been watching the bank at Kentish Town. In due course, one of the gang was seen approaching. He was arrested, and the keys of the bank and a watch belonging to Deans were found on him. Eventually five other men were arrested, and sentenced to terms of penal servitude ranging from three to seven years.

One of the most interesting cases handled by the Flying Squad since the war was that of Bert Holliday. It illustrates perhaps better than any other the way in which some small item of information may set off an inquiry, the detailed and untiring work of investigation, and how, in spite of their independent status, four police forces co-operated in bringing to an end a long series of burglaries in the Home Counties. It also illustrates the necessity of that occasional stroke of luck without which the most patient detective work would often be unavailing.

The inquiry began in November, 1947, when the Flying Squad was working with the Surrey Constabulary on a series of burglaries in Surrey. Information came in that the receiver would be found living on the Thames near Weybridge. Two known criminals were quickly identified in that area, and were closely watched. One was fairly soon eliminated, it being obvious that he had no connection with the robberies being investigated. The other, perhaps fortunately from the point of view of the police, died before much time had been wasted on following a false trail.

115

Then came the first stroke of luck. In February, 1949, Chief Inspector Tomlin, of the Buckinghamshire Constabulary, was called in to inquire into the theft of a cheese from the Dumb Bell Hotel at Taplow. Two men had entered the bar and called for drinks. The potman had his back turned towards them and, looking in the mirror, saw one of the men take a cheese and hide it inside his coat. I should dearly love to know – and so would Superintendent Lee of the Flying Squad – what prompted the man to steal the cheese. He was known locally as Bertram Redvers Holliday, and he lived in a bungalow called 'Jour de Fête' on an island in the Thames at Wraysbury. When Chief Inspector Tomlin called upon him, Holliday, who described himself as a property owner and jeweller, denied that he knew anything about the missing cheese. The Chief Inspector felt, however, that he would repay investigation, and passed his suspicions on to Superintendent Lee.

At first the name Bertram Redvers Holliday conveyed nothing to Superintendent Lee; but later information that he was called Bert Holliday rang a bell, for Lee had known Bert Holliday well some twenty-four years before, when he had been an extremely active burglar. A search in the Criminal Record Office soon produced full details of Holliday's earlier career. Since that time, however, he had not come to the notice of the police, and had been living a life of apparent affluence and respectability.

The man who had originally given the information about the receiver's whereabouts was interviewed again, and said that Holliday was the man he suspected. But he refused to say any more, and the police were left to carry on with their inquiries. For over three months they kept Holliday under continuous observation; but beyond the fact that he had left the bungalow and moved to London, where he had taken a flat in Earl's Court Square, they discovered nothing. Later, the Flying Squad's information stated that Holliday had left a lot of valuable jewellery in a safe deposit. Inquiries were made at every safe deposit in London, but none could be found which was rented by Holliday. What did come to light, however, was that in 1946 Holliday had transferred a heavy deed box from a bank in Windsor to his wife's bank in Chelsea.

The next scrap of information added a spice of urgency to the search, for it was learned that Holliday was not merely a receiver, but also an expert climber who, with an accomplice,

116

was carrying out a series of burglaries. A watch was now set on the accomplice, too, but he was very elusive. After a while, however, news reached the police of an intended robbery on September 8. On that day, Holliday and his accomplice were to meet near Osterley Park Station, on the Great West Road. The police waited at the rendezvous, and presently Holliday's car was seen to pull up. As soon as his accomplice had got in, Holliday drove off on the wrong side of the road at high speed, going towards London. He then turned and made off towards Staines. This manoeuvre shook off the police officers, but as no crime was reported that night, there was nothing to be done except wait for another chance.

It came fairly soon, when information was received about another intended burglary. This time it was to be at Wraysbury on October 14. The police were early on the scene, but Holliday and his friend were there even earlier, and having seen the police officers arrive, they made off again.

The next piece of information the police received was that a certain bookmaker, known as Poofy Len, might be worth their attention. Poofy Len was quickly identified as a man named Oades. Watch was kept on him, and on December 13 he and Holliday were seen together at Earl's Court Square. They drove in Oades' car to Mrs Holliday's bank in Chelsea, and soon afterwards Holliday came out carrying a brown-paper parcel. The detectives of the Flying Squad seized their opportunity. Taking a chance that the parcel contained stolen goods, they stopped and searched the two men and the car. Inside the parcel were several pieces of valuable jewellery, which Holliday claimed as his own. Oades, who denied that he knew anything about it, was found at the police station to have on him five petrol coupons, which he admitted had been got illegally. He was therefore detained.

The police next visited Mrs Holliday's bank, from which they collected a suitcase and the deed box deposited there by Holliday in his wife's name in 1946. The box, which had contained the jewellery found in his parcel, was now empty, but in the suitcase was a collection of silver plate and some cutlery. The cutlery was claimed by Mrs Holliday, though she denied any knowledge of the silver.

Meanwhile, in the presence of Mrs Holliday and Mrs Oades, the two men's homes were searched. At Earl's Court Square, the police found an enormous collection of valuables of all

117

kinds. At Oades' address in Hounslow was a wall safe containing some precious stones and jewellery. In the time available it was not possible to identify any of the silver or jewellery, though widespread inquiries were in progress. But the police felt sure enough of their ground to charge Holliday with unlawful possession of the jewellery found in his car. The next day he and Oades were brought before the magistrate at West London Police Court, and remanded on bail of £2,000. A few minutes later came the news that one of the articles in the suitcase, an inscribed silver cup, was identical with one stolen from a house in Stoke Poges in 1946. Upon this, Mrs Holliday was arrested, charged with receiving the cup, and remanded to appear with her husband and Oades at the next hearing.

After his release on bail, Oades was escorted by the police to a safe deposit, and in his safe more jewellery was found. By December 16, a fair amount of the property seized by the police in Holliday's flat had been identified as the proceeds of various big robberies in Buckinghamshire.

The police, still keeping their ears to the ground, learned that Holliday was very worried about the property already seized and had made plans to dispose of some more which he had hidden. He was again watched – though not without difficulty – and early on the morning of December 18 he was followed from his flat to Staines; but in the deserted streets it was impossible to keep close to him without being seen, and in Staines the trail was lost. For three days he completely disappeared. Then, on December 21, the police at Egham, near Staines, reported that a man had been found shot through the head at a hotel at Virginia Water. The man was Bertram Holliday. If, between December 18 and 21, he had succeeded in disposing of other stolen property, he took the secret with him, for none has since been discovered.

When all the articles that had been seized were assembled, they were laid out at Scotland Yard for inspection by possible claimants. Lists and photographs were widely published, police records were searched, and people who had been robbed were invited to come to Scotland Yard to see if they could identify their property. A remarkable display awaited them – guns, compasses, microscopes, statuary, plate, watches, clocks and jewellery testified to the catholic tastes of the 'Gentleman Cracksman', as the papers called Holliday.

In the end, seventeen items were identified as the proceeds of burglaries dating from 1932 to 1949, which had taken place in London and various parts of Surrey, Berkshire and Buckinghamshire. The rest of the property was never identified, and as Mrs Holliday disclaimed any right to it, it was eventually sold and the proceeds given to the Prisoners' Property Fund, from which payments are made from time to time, under the authority of the Home Secretary, to various police charities and discharged prisoners' aid societies.

Much of Holliday's loot no doubt remains undiscovered, but in spite of an intensive search by the Flying Squad and their colleagues in the County Constabularies, nothing more has been found except a valuable diamond brooch. This was concealed in a telephone receiver, and discovered after a chance remark by Mrs Holliday that she had once seen her husband 'fiddling about with the telephone' in an odd way.

It was obvious as the inquiry went on that Mrs Holliday had been entirely under the influence of her husband, and when she came up for trial the jury took this into account and found her not guilty of receiving. Although full lists and photographs of the property seized from Oades had been widely circulated, it was impossible to identify any as having been stolen, and Oades was therefore dealt with only in respect of the petrol coupons, and fined five pounds for possessing them.

So ended one of the most audacious careers to be found even in the records of the Flying Squad. In their pursuit of Holliday, the detectives faced considerable risks, for he always carried a gun on his housebreaking expeditions, and at his bedside an automatic pistol was found, with several hundred rounds of ammunition. A less obvious risk was that which they took when they stopped and searched Holliday and Oades on suspicion, for a wrongful arrest can lead to a claim against the police for fairly heavy compensation. Every year the police stop about 70,000 people, of whom some ninety per cent turn out to be innocent. It is a tribute to police handling of these cases – and to the common sense of the public – that I never received more than four or five complaints a year, out of which came two or three claims for compensation, and these we were generally able to settle out of court. Without this right to stop and search, however, it is obvious that many such clever criminals as Holliday would never be caught.

Wartime restrictions added greatly to the work of the police, and none more than the various rationing orders. The offenders were mostly small fry who tried to evade the orders and obtain for themselves a little more than their ration. But from time to time information reached the police of operations on a grander scale, in which clever groups of criminals applied their skill to the forging and distribution of coupons of one kind or another. This new type of crime was a challenge to the Flying Squad, and they met it with characteristic energy and persistence. In January, 1948, for instance, the Minister of Fuel and Power set up a committee, under the chairmanship of Sir Godfrey Russell Vick, to devise a foolproof scheme for rationing petrol. Chief Superintendent Chapman, who was then head of the Flying Squad, was seconded to the committee for several weeks, and the chairman told me afterwards that his wide knowledge of the dealings in blackmarket petrol contributed very considerably to the introduction of the red petrol scheme.

One of the most lucrative frauds during and after the war was the forging of clothing coupons, since clothes rationing was the form of restriction most severely felt and the one from which the greatest gains were to be realised. At one time as much as forty guineas was being paid for a thousand forged coupons. In 1947 the Board of Trade became gravely perturbed at the scale on which forged coupons were circulating, and asked Scotland Yard to undertake an investigation into the source. The Flying Squad soon received information that a woman named Burns was associating with the forger and was herself one of the principal distributors. She was followed for many weeks, and was seen to pass forged coupons. She was not arrested, however, because it was hoped that she would eventually lead the detectives to the source of the coupons. In time it became known that she was connected with a man named William Roberts, alias Watson, who had many convictions for coining and one for being in possession of a plate for making ten-shilling notes. He had come out of prison in 1944, and since then he and the woman Burns had often been seen together.

When at last Watson was traced to an address in Maida Vale, search warrants were obtained and simultaneous raids were made on the homes of Watson and Burns, and a couple named Hefferman, whom they had been seen to visit. When the Squad arrived at Watson's address, the door was locked. There was no answer when they knocked, so they forced an entry. Inside they found Watson who, when he saw the game was up and that the evidence in the room was inescapable, admitted that he was responsible for making the forged coupons. The room was, in fact, a fully equipped workshop, in which the police found photographic plates with prints of fifteen clothing coupons, copper printing plates and a stock of paper with multiple water-marks showing the insignia of the Stationery Office and a crown. On a table was a hand-press, and in the corner a darkened cubicle. Among other apparatus were a camera and slides, a paper-trimmer, drawing-boards and engraving tools – in fact, the whole paraphernalia required for high-class forgery.

On a table near the bed was found a wallet containing forty sheets of forged clothing coupons, When they were shown to Watson he said with some pride, 'You don't want me to tell you where they came from. They aren't a bad job, are they?' When he was cautioned and told he would be arrested he said philosophically, 'That's fair enough.

The officers who had gone to Burn's home in Notting Hill found twenty sheets of forged coupons. She tried to suggest that they could have been planted on her, but later, when arrested, she said, 'I must be mad to get mixed up with Watson – I know there are thousands of these coupons in Kensington.'

Mrs Hefferman, too, seemed to regret her husband's choice of associates, for when she and her husband were told that they would be arrested they began arguing among themselves, and Mrs Hefferman said, 'This is what comes of mixing with those people.' There were ten more sheets of forged coupons at their house.

All four were committed for trial at the Central Criminal Court. Watson was sentenced to seven years' penal servitude for making and possessing forged coupons, and Burns and Hefferman to twelve months' imprisonment for possessing them. Mrs Hefferman was found not guilty.

This was a first-class Flying Squad effort by a team of eleven officers, including a woman police sergeant, under Detective Inspector George Robinson. For eight weeks they watched continuously, often going without meals, and had the satisfaction of breaking up an expert forging gang who were the focus of a country-wide evasion of the rationing scheme.

To the outside observer it must probably seem, often quite correctly, that the police know a man, or a group of men, to be engaged in crime; but from lack of evidence they are sometimes unable to bring a case to court. They must then play a waiting game until convincing evidence comes into their hands, as it usually does.

In 1946, the Flying Squad had been watching a dangerous gang whose members were suspected of smash-and-grab raids. The Squad had strong suspicions about them, but insufficient evidence to make arrests. Then early one morning a uniformed policeman patrolling in the Clerkenwell area, saw a car with five or six men in it turn from a side road into a main road against the red light. An hour later the same car reappeared, travelling very fast in the opposite direction, and on it the officer saw a large 'N' in black on a white ground. Convinced that something was wrong, he followed the track of the car on the wet road until he saw it coming towards him again. He stepped out into the road and flashed his torch as a signal to stop, but the car was driven on at high speed, and as it drew level with him there was a flash and a loud report, as of a gun, from the front seat. He was, however, unhurt. The car, a Royal Norwegian Army vehicle which had been stolen the night before, was later found abandoned in Rosebery Avenue, near the scene of the shooting. In it was a label from a fur coat, one of £2,500 worth stolen during the night from a furrier's shop in Mount Street.

Acting on information they had gathered, Flying Squad officers went that evening to an address in Clerkenwell, where a suspect named King had a bedroom. King was out, but in an overcoat pocket the officers found a Mauser automatic and several rounds of ammunition. Under the bedclothes were a Lüger automatic, a jemmy, six bunches of car keys, more ammunition, a knuckle-duster, a dagger in a sheath, and an Underground railway strap-hanger with a rubber ball on the end. The same evening, officers also visited a house in St Pancras occupied by a Mrs Ward and her daughter. There they found three Persian lamb coats, eleven other fur coats, and four revolvers with twenty-one rounds of ammunition. Mrs Ward protested that the coats belonged to her lodger and said she knew nothing of the revolvers, which must also belong to him. Nevertheless, she and her daughter were arrested for receiving, and taken to King's Cross Police Station.

Officers were waiting at the Clerkenwell address, and in time another suspect, named Papworth, appeared. He was asked about the raid in Mount Street and answered jauntily, 'Not me,

I'm not worried.' However, he too was arrested, and when he reached the police station he said, 'Who bubbled? If they bubbled I'll tell my side.' He then made a statement that he had met the team at the Strand Corner House, and agreed to drive a car and 'do a fur job' in the West End. He denied having fired at the policeman, but admitted breaking the window of the fur shop and driving the car away.

It was now the suspect King's turn. He was found and asked about the Mount Street raid. 'Somebody's had a real good bubble,' was his reply. 'If they've put me in, I'll get them. I'll tell you what I know about it.'

He was cautioned and detained, and later made a statement in which he said that Mrs Ward and her daughter were innocent. He had been staying in the Clerkenwell bedroom for a month, using the bed where the Lüger was found. He had bought it and the Mauser found in his overcoat pocket from two Canadian soldiers. He then described how the gang broke the window of the shop in Mount Street, took the furs and drove away. They left the furs at Mrs Ward's house, where he knew the daughter and had a key. While they were driving the car away with the intention of abandoning it, a policeman shone his torch, and the man sitting next to the driver fired a shot to scare him off taking the car number. After they had abandoned the car, the gang split up, and King had returned to his bedroom and hidden the two guns.

The police next saw another suspect named Vigors, who admitted that he had been at Mount Street and had put the furs in the back of the car. But he denied the shooting, which he alleged had been done by King. He also implicated another two men named Rawson and Morgan, neither of whom could be found for nearly three weeks. When finally the police cornered them in the same block of buildings as King's room, Morgan tried to get rid of a knuckleduster, but it was seized. Both men made statements, and were afterwards charged.

Meanwhile, King had described an earlier burglary, when the gang had stolen gowns from a shop in Holloway Road. While they were forcing the lock of another shop on the same night, a police car arrived and gave chase. Fog had made it impossible to drive fast enough to shake off the police car, so King had smashed the rear window and fired a shot at the bonnet of the police car as a warning. The driver took no notice, so he fired at the tyres, and the police car pulled up and

123

put out its lights. Two hundred yards further on, King's car had broken down, so they abandoned it.

When the police had found the abandoned car there were in it fifty-two dresses, a jemmy, a wrench and two point thirty-two cartridge cases. On the front door were King's fingerprints. The cartridge cases from that incident, and from the later shooting in Clerkenwell, had been examined by Mr Churchill, the ballistics expert, who had reported that they had all been fired by the Mauser pistol found in King's overcoat. The furs found at the Wards' were identified as stolen by the owner of the Mount Street shop.

The five men and the two Wards were tried at the Central Criminal Court, where Rawson and the two women were found not guilty. There was, however, no doubt about the guilt of the other men, and after conviction King confessed to his share in the shooting, and admitted another smash-and-grab raid in New Bond Street. So ended, for the time being, the activities of an exceedingly troublesome gang.

Chapter 12
THE FRAUD SQUAD

THE more spectacular crimes of violence so prevalent after the war overshadowed the fact that there was also a spate of frauds in the launching of bogus companies or the conduct of existing ones. Investigation of fraud, especially of company fraud, is a highly specialised business, calling for a knowledge of company law and accountancy that the average C.I.D. officer does not possess. There was at Scotland Yard, however, a small group of officers, who had had considerable experience of this kind of inquiry, and in March, 1946, we formed them into the nucleus of a new Company Fraud Department. As this type of crime often involved inquiries not only in the Metropolitan Police District but also in the City of London, I suggested to Sir Hugh Turnbull, the Commissioner of Police for the City, that it would be a good thing to form a joint department composed of officers of both forces. He readily agreed, and so for the first time Metropolitan and City Police embarked on combined operations.

This, incidentally, brought to light an anomaly which had passed unnoticed for many years. Under the Metropolitan Police Act of 1839, Metropolitan Police officers 'may execute the office of constable within the royal palaces of Her Majesty and ten miles thereof,' which, of course, includes the City of London; but there is no similar enactment authorising City Police officers to exercise their powers outside their own area. City Police officers attached to the Fraud Squad began investigating a case in the City Area which, after some months, extended over the boundary into the Metropolitan Police District. The case papers went in due course to the Director of Public Prosecutions, and application for a warrant was made at Clerkenwell Court. Such warrants are addressed 'to each and all of the Constables of the Metropolitan Police Force', and, as a consequence, hasty arrangements had to be made for a Metropolitan Police officer in the Fraud Squad to make the application, execute the warrant, and then to give evidence of arrest in a case about which he knew precisely nothing. The City Commissioner was advised that if his officers attached to the Fraud Squad had power of arrest in the Metropolitan Police area, there would be no difficulty, and he agreed to five of his officers being sworn in as Metropolitan Police Officers. The position has now been regularised by Act of Parliament.

The Company Fraud Department was placed from its beginning under the leadership of Chief Superintendent Thorp, who retired in 1954. In its first year the Squad handled 290 cases, and every year the number has steadily increased. Quite apart from those which have been taken into court, its inquiries have nipped in the bud many promising schemes which, if they had been allowed to go on, might have been as profitable to their promoters as they would have been unprofitable to the public.

Many cases originate from the Squad's own inquiries. Others are referred to it by the Board of Trade, the Customs and other Government departments, and provincial forces frequently ask it to take over complicated cases for them. It was obviously very desirable that in the larger towns such as Manchester, Liverpool, Bristol and Brighton, a small number of officers should be available to work on similar lines, and to co-operate with the Squad. I therefore agreed with the Chief Constables concerned that some of their officers should be attached to the Squad to learn its methods and gain experience, and these officers are now operating in their own towns.

The most famous of the Fraud Squad's inquiries was that which led to the Lynskey Tribunal of 1948. In that year rumours were widely circulated that certain Ministers and civil servants had been induced by payments, gifts or other considerations to show favours to certain applicants for the licences or permission they required. On July 2, Superintendent Thorp began investigations with one assistant. Before the end of the inquiry, fifteen extra detectives had to be seconded to the Squad, and he himself interviewed and took statements from several hundred people. The Squad's preliminary inquiries indicated that in some cases the allegations of corruption might be well founded, and as a result a Tribunal was set up, under Mr Justice Lynskey, and sat for nearly a month hearing evidence. As a result most of the allegations were shown to be quite unfounded and the names of those concerned were cleared. In two cases, however, the Tribunal reported that favours had been improperly sought and granted, and though there was nothing on which criminal proceedings could be based, the report led to the resignation of the two persons concerned. The Squad was warmly commended by the Tribunal for its work in this painful case, and there can be no doubt that it served as a most useful warning and did much to affirm the need for scrupulous avoidance of any relationship between officers of the Crown and those who have business dealings with them, which might give rise to suspicions of undue influence.

Another case which took months of inquiry was that of George Eric Titley, a chartered accountant who had converted to his own use some £30,000 due to a road haulage firm for which he acted, when the firm was nationalised. He had also converted £2,900 which he obtained through selling a leather company on behalf of the late managing director's widow. The Squad's report on this case dealt with an intricate series of transactions in which a clever rogue had sought to cover up his fraudulent dealings, and an officer was eventually sent out to Queensland, to which Titley had gone, to bring him back. He was later sentenced to seven years' imprisonment.

Occasionally the work of the Squad leads it into very different fields, as, for example, in 1950, when it investigated the substitution of an Irish horse, Newton Rock, which had raced very successfully in Ireland, for a brown gelding, Liffey Valley. Liffey Valley, after a short and unsuccessful career in Ireland, was sold to a Birmingham bookmaker and was never seen again. Newton Rock, however, ran in England as Liffey Valley in maiden novice races, with success and at long odds, but inquiry by the Squad put an end to his career and that of his buyer at the Central Criminal Court in February, 1951.

Another substitution was that of Stellar City for Peaceful William. Stellar City, a brown Irish colt which had won races in Ireland in 1949, was brought to England and won a number of races as Peaceful William until September of that year. Rumours began to spread and the Jockey Club became interested. Stellar City had a white star on his forehead which Peaceful William had not, and to hide it a special leather medallion was fitted to his noseband. Unluckily for his owner, the medallion slipped when the horse was being led in after a win at Lanark, and a press photograph made a permanent record of the star. The Squad duly collected the evidence, and two men were sentenced to eighteen months' imprisonment on seven counts of fraud.

As with horses, so with dogs. Substitution of an older, more experienced dog for a younger gives the owner an unfair advantage. In October, 1949, an anonymous letter was received at Scotland Yard alleging that a dog called Red Wind, which had been very successful in recent races in London, was a much older Irish dog named Waggles. In England, every litter of greyhounds must be registered with the National Coursing Club, and particulars must be given of its sire and dam, colour, markings including even the colours of its toenails, and within two years each puppy must be named. If the dog is to race, particulars must also be registered with the National Greyhound Racing Club, who issue an identity card on which a record of all races is entered. In June, 1948, a greyhound owner registered five puppies in England, and in September one of them was named Red Wind. In his racing trials in July, 1949, Red Wind did only moderately. Yet two days after the last trial, he ran 500 yards in less time than he had previously taken to run 460. He then proceeded to win a whole series of major races, many of them in record time. When the Fraud Squad looked into the matter, they found that an older dog named Waggles, which had raced successfully in Ireland, had been brought to England by aeroplane in May, 1949, and sold to a man in Edgware for over £1,000. The Fraud Squad brought witnesses from Ireland to England, who examined the so-called 'Red Wind', and had no difficulty in identifying him as the dog they had known in Ireland as Waggles. The Squad's inquiries produced evidence of other substitutions, and the owner and his brother were sentenced at the Central Criminal Court to two years' and eighteen months' imprisonment respectively.

But such cases form the lighter side of the Fraud Squad's work, and it has been in the commercial field that their activities have been of the greatest value. Here the Squad has fully justified its creation, and the development of this very specialised form of detective work has done much to clean up a most unsavoury aspect of our business life.

Chapter 13
THE BLACK MUSEUM

RELICS of famous crimes have always exercised a curious fascination over all sorts of people, and the Black Museum at Scotland Yard has a reputation far beyond police circles. It began as a collection of exhibits from famous trials which, after they had been shown in court, were dumped in a room in the basement. To this room favoured visitors were taken by members of the C.I.D., and the approach through dark and dusty underground passages added a spice of excitement to the visit. If the detective was a good story-teller – as they mostly are – he described the exhibits and their history in such a way that the visitor's blood was well and truly curdled.

I first visited the Museum when I was at the Home Office, and found it a rather grubby place housing a haphazard collection of objects of morbid interest, unadapted for any training purpose. That was provided by the Museum at the Detective Training School at Hendon, a collection of a different type which had been created for the instruction of students. During the war, the exhibits in the Black Museum were pushed aside to make room for more important activities. When the war was over it seemed to me that it would be worth while to reinstate the Black Museum, but in a form which, while preserving the macabre interest of the old collection, would, like the Detective School Museum, include exhibits for the instruction of visiting police officers and other people interested in various aspects of crime. The Museum is still in the basement, though, to the regret of some who remember it as it was, it is no longer a place of dirt and grime. It has been remodelled and redecorated, new lighting has been installed, and special showcases designed. In this new setting the collection has lost none of its interest, and it shows one, as nothing else could, the infinite variety of criminal behaviour.

Around the walls is a collection of death masks of prisoners hanged in Newgate Prison. These were taken for the purpose of phrenological research at a time when Lombroso's theory of a criminal type was accepted by many criminologists. This theory was disproved over fifty years ago by the researches of an English Prison Medical Officer, Dr Goring, but the death masks remain as a reminder of the time when the problem of the criminal seemed far simpler than it does today. Of modern masks, that of Himmler, the chief of Hitler's Gestapo, finds an appropriate place in this curious gallery. It was brought to the museum by a Metropolitan Police officer who was serving in the Public Safety Department in Germany at the time of Himmler's capture.

In the first room there is a unique collection of housebreaking instruments, showing the ingenious and elaborate equipment of the professional burglar, together with specimens of coshes and other weapons used by criminals. One of the most interesting of these exhibits belonged to Charles Peace who, after a long career of housebreaking, was hanged at Armley Gaol, Leeds, on February 25, 1879, for the murder of Mrs Dyson. It includes his chisel, gouge and gimlet, a small vice, picklocks and skeleton keys, a lantern made from a match-box, dark glasses and a false arm which he used as a disguise, a crucible for melting down stolen jewellery, and his ladder, made of rope with wooden rungs, which could be folded into a small compass and carried to the scene of operations.

Another exhibit is a walking stick. During 1952, the police had been troubled by a series of burglaries in which the thief had always got in through an upper window. One foggy night in December of that year, a young constable on duty near the Dorchester Hotel saw a man trying the doors of some of the cars parked nearby. When the constable ran towards him, he made off towards Hyde Park, but was overtaken and caught at the fence. There, he dropped the walking-stick on the pavement, and later drew an automatic pistol from his pocket and threw it away. Afterwards it was found that under his trousers he had a sharp knife strapped to his leg, and a jemmy suspended from his braces. His equipment was completed by a small torch with a spare battery, nine bolts, and a large piece of silk stocking placed round his neck so that it could instantly be pulled over his face.

Examination of the walking-stick showed how he had been able to get into the upper windows. The 'stick' consists of five telescopic tubes which, when pulled out, form a pole about eleven feet long. At intervals of about a foot there are transverse holes through which the nine bolts can be pushed to form the rungs of a ladder, which could then be hooked on to a ledge or balcony by means of the crooked handle, which was covered with rubberised tape. Only its weight gave an indication that this ingenious piece of apparatus was not what it purported to be, and an artistic touch was the addition of a rubber ferrule to give it the appearance of an invalid's stick. The prisoner had a long record of serious convictions, and on his pleading guilty to possessing a firearm without lawful excuse when loitering with intent to commit a felony, he was sentenced to ten years' preventive detention.

Nearby is the equipment of 'Flannelfoot', a housebreaker who for years successfully avoided the police and carried out his thefts all over London. He usually worked on Saturday or Sunday, and entered several adjoining small houses on the same night. His method was either to push back the window latch with some sharp instrument, or to remove the putty and take out the window-pane, or else to manipulate the door key by means of a pair of fine pliers. He left no fingerprints, and either wore galoshes or covered his feet with cloth so as to move silently and leave no shoe prints. He usually took a bicycle and rode away to a railway station or a tram route, where he abandoned the bicycle and took an early-morning train or tram back to central London.

From 1933 to 1936, in spite of intensive inquiry and the use of large numbers of plain clothes men, Flannelfoot continued to operate with impunity, and it was then decided to set up a special squad to deal with this persistent burglar. The Map Room plotted all suspected cases on a special map, linking them with the places where the bicycles were abandoned, and the squad studied the map with care and followed up every clue. All the criminals who were known to use a similar method were kept under observation until all but one were eliminated. This was a man named Edward Vicars, who had had only one conviction, some twenty years before.

Hundreds of police were employed in a widespread search which at last led to the discovery of Vicars' address. But he was very elusive and quick to sense if he was being followed, sometimes turning into a *cul-de-sac* for no other reason than to find out if anyone was shadowing him.

A flat opposite his house was rented and a team of officers, including some women, watched in relays along various routes, sometimes using cars or taxis to follow him. Eventually, in October, 1937, the long search ended. Flannelfoot was followed by bus and train to Eastcote station, in the western suburbs, and though he disappeared in the darkness, he was found after a time coming from the garden of an unoccupied house. He was carrying a whole collection of housebreaking implements, and when his house was searched the police found the proceeds of several burglaries. In the face of this evidence he admitted about forty offences, but he would only admit cases where it was clear that the police were in a position to prove him guilty. It was estimated that in 1937 alone, he was responsible for no fewer than 135 housebreakings, and he had been operating on a similar scale since 1933, if not earlier. After his arrest, offences of this kind almost ceased, and there was no recurrence.

In the museum is preserved his working kit, including a pair of galoshes, a pair of leather gloves, a collection of keys, pieces of plasticine for taking the impressions of keys, a bit-holder and two wooden bits, a pair of pliers, a metal tubular grip, some wire, a table-knife, and the feet of a pair of socks which he wore over his shoes and from which he gained the name of 'Flannelfoot'.

One exhibit in the museum illustrates the importance of overlooking nothing, however trivial, that may be found at the scene of a crime. It is a broken button discovered on the window-sill of a house entered by a man who was later detained on suspicion of housebreaking and attempted murder. One of the buttons on his coat was broken, and the piece found on the window-sill exactly fitted the broken button. On this evidence he was convicted.

Of similar significance are some wedges, and some wooden chair legs. The wedges were found in certain houses where burglaries had been committed. When the home of the suspected burglar was searched, it was found that the wedges exactly fitted chair legs there, from which they had been cut. Also in this section are some of the clock-bombs used by the I.R.A. at the time of the Irish troubles during and after the first world war, together with the uniform, sword, tobacco box and other relics of Sir Roger Casement, who was executed in 1916 for treason.

The second section of the museum is devoted mainly to the coiner's art, but with the disappearance of the golden sovereign and the debasement of the silver coinage, counterfeiting of

132

coins has largely died out. More important today is the art of forgery, for which the opportunities have been enormously widened by the great increase in documents of value, other than banknotes, that are now in everyday use. Cheques, postal orders, savings bank books, insurance stamps, season tickets and many other documents offer a lucrative field to the forger. Some of the best forgeries of Bank of England notes are those printed in Nazi Germany and circulated during the war, but there are also hand-drawn notes which almost defy detection. When examining some of these, I could not help wondering if they were the work of a skilful forger who, in my early days at the Home Office, was found to have got permission to practise engraving while he was serving a sentence of penal servitude in Portland Prison; or of the prison librarian I met many years later, serving a sentence of preventive detention in Portsmouth Prison. He was a courteous and scholarly old gentleman and a most valuable librarian. We discussed his history, and he explained to me with regret that he had come to the conclusion that forgery was an unremunerative occupation, 'for,' said he, 'the overhead expenses are too high.'

They must certainly have been high for the man who forged the three-and-sixpenny postal order exhibited in one of the cases. He had changed the '3' to '8' in the large figures denoting the value of the order. Then he had laboriously changed the word 'three' to 'eight' many times over, in the repeated lettering that surrounds the central panel. Unfortunately for him, he forgot to change the value of the poundage stamp at the side, and it was this that gave the game away.

In this section of the Museum are specimens of mock jewellery used by confidence tricksters, and gambling contrivances used by swindlers, such as a roulette wheel that can be stopped at will by the operator, card shoes and the like.

The card shoe or holder, used in *chemin de fer,* is rather like a shovel with sides to it. There is a metal piece at the front with a slot, through which the cards are passed out one at a time, and a block which slides up and down the length of the shoe and keeps the cards in place. There is no trick about the shoe itself; in fact quite the opposite. It is intended to ensure that only the top card of the pack can be dealt out. The pack of cards which go into the shoe are apparently new and sealed, but one or more have previously been opened, stacked in a certain sequence, and resealed. When the card sharpers have secured their victim, the packs are opened and shuffled, although, of course, the rigged packs are given a false shuffle so that the sequence of the cards is not altered. The tricksters take no part in the game until a prearranged signal is given – the draw of a certain card – that the rigged cards are coming out of the shoe. It is arranged by this time that the victim, holding the shoe, is banker, and he is well fleeced.

The gullibility of some people is beyond belief. So, too, perhaps, is their confidence in their ability to get something for nothing. An ingenious dodge by which a gang of Australian swindlers cleared large sums of money was the Gold Brick Fraud, which is illustrated by a specimen of the 'gold' brick. Some innocent in a bar or hotel lounge would find himself in conversation with a stranger who, for some specious reason, had to sell a boxful of gold bars at, of course, a bargain rate. The stranger, as a measure of his trust, was perfectly willing to leave a specimen with the buyer, and this, if assayed, proved to be of gold. All the other bars in the box, which the buyer rarely bothered to examine closely, weighed as much as gold. But they were in fact bars of brass with tubes of mercury inserted in the centre to bring the weights up to the required level.

In the Museum, too, is a collection of bags and cases specially constructed for use by smugglers and shoplifters. In those used by smugglers, double sides and bottoms, as well as other contrivances, are cunningly concealed to deceive the customs officers. The cases used by shoplifters have either hinged ends, through which stolen articles can be pushed by hand, or hinged bottoms. This device allows the cases to be put down on top of the article that is going to be stolen, so that when the shoplifter picks up the case again, the article is inside it.

In the third section of the Museum are relics of many famous murder cases. There are, for example, P.C. Edgar's pocket book with the entry he was making when he was shot, the rubber truncheon belonging to Thomas, his murderer, various bullets and bullet cases, and the book, *Shooting to Live,* which was found on Thomas. Nearby are the raincoat and revolvers referred to in the d'Antiquis case, and pieces of the bloodstained floorboards from the flat of Douglas Hume, who was convicted for being an accessory to the murder of Stanley Setty. Older cases are recalled by the revolver used by Udham Singh in the assassination of Sir Michael O'Dwyer on the platform at Caxton Hall in 1940; the rolling pin, pistol and other articles belonging to Ronald True, who was sentenced to death in May, 1922, for the murder of Gertrude Yates, but later found insane and sent to Broadmoor; the hunting-knife used by Bywaters in the murder for which he and Mrs Thompson were convicted in December, 1922; the diaries of Herbert Armstrong, the South Wales solicitor, and two packets of arsenic similar to those he used for poisoning his wife in 1922; the medicine chest and stethoscope used by Neill Cream, the Lambeth poisoner, who was hanged at Newgate for the murder of Matilda Clover by administering strychnine; and a number of relics of the Crippen case of 1910, including the wireless telegram which led to the arrest of Crippen and his companion, Ethel le Neve, on their arrival at New York. This, incidentally, was the first time wireless had ever been used for such a purpose.

Another interesting set of exhibits is that connected with the murder of P.C. Gutteridge, of the Essex Constabulary, by Browne and Kennedy in 1928. They include the running-board and mudguard of the car which was stolen from a doctor, with the bloodstains caused by the shooting; a number of the surgical instruments missing from the car, when it was found abandoned in Brixton, which were later discovered in Browne's garage nearby; two face-masks worn by the criminals; and two revolvers, one of which was found on Browne when he was arrested and was proved to have been used to fire a cartridge case left in the stolen car.

The Museum also contains a number of exhibits illustrating the history of the Metropolitan Police, but partly because of a wholesale destruction of records and other mementos at the time of the move to the present building in 1890, they are comparatively few in number.

Chapter 14

THE SPECIAL BRANCH AND VISIT OF
MARSHAL TITO

THE difference between our conception of the role of the
police and that of many other countries was brought home to
me quite soon after I went to Scotland Yard by a conversation
I had with the Director-General of the Sûreté in Paris. He
asked if I often saw the Home Secretary, and I told him that
apart from social occasions, I might go for a month or more
without seeing him, although, of course, my office conducted
a regular official correspondence with the Home Office on
administrative matters. He was very astonished, '*Mon Dieu*,'
he said. 'I see *my* Minister for two hours every morning.'

There is, in fact, nothing in common between the Metropolitan Police, or even the Special Branch, and the political
police as they are understood in many other countries. The
Special Branch is a part of the Criminal Investigation Department, and is primarily an intelligence department. Its business
is to keep a watch on any body of people, of whatever political
complexion, whose activities seem likely to result sooner or
later in open acts of sedition or disorder. Thus from time to
time it has been concerned with the Irish Republican Brother-
hood, whose dynamite outrages in 1884 brought the Branch
into existence, Sinn Fein, Fascists, Communists, anarchists,
suffragettes, Indian nationalists and, during wartime, intelligence agents of enemy powers.

At its head was formerly Commander L. J. Burt, M.V.O.,
who began his career on the beat as a uniformed constable,
joined the C.I.D., and during the second world war was lent to
M.I.5 for duty. He came back to Scotland Yard in 1945, as head
of the Special Branch. Burt was characteristic of his branch
inasmuch as he was a quiet, imperturbable man whom one
might take for a higher civil servant or a university don rather
than a policeman. He had a remarkable memory, and an
encyclopaedic knowledge of the curious people who have engaged in subversive movements for very many years.

Special Branch officers have no powers beyond those of the ordinary police officer, and if action has to be taken it is usually left to the ordinary branches of the force. A representative of the Special Branch is stationed at every port and airport, and it is his duty, in co-operation with the Immigration Officer, to scrutinise closely all aliens who wish to enter the country. A knowledge of languages and an interest in the byways of political thought and action are required of the officers of this branch, but they are so often credited with much more sinister activities that it is only fair to say that, if such activities exist, I have failed to discover them, though I have worked closely with Special Branch officers for most of the last forty years.

Another duty of the Special Branch is to provide officers for the protection of Ministers. It is a long time since any attempt was made on the life of a Minister in this country, and it is seldom necessary to afford protection to any but the Prime Minister, the Home Secretary and the Foreign Secretary, who are the most prominent members of the Government and the most likely targets for trouble-makers. The officers' main duty is to save Ministers from being molested or annoyed, but they must always be on the watch for something more serious and be prepared to deal with it or to call in the assistance of other officers if it is needed.

Similar protection is also given to heads of foreign States or other important visitors from abroad. In November, 1952, for instance, the Home Secretary asked for my view on the possibility of making adequate security arrangements if Marshal Tito came on an official visit to this country. I felt bound to say that there was a risk which must not be underestimated, but that we would do our best, though it was, of course, impossible to guarantee that nothing untoward would happen. I had in mind that there was a grim history of political assassination in the Marshal's country. If some fanatical opponent could make his way into this country under the guise of a visitor or a student, and was prepared to face the consequences of his act, he might well try to take advantage of our free and easy ways to attempt a crime that would be more difficult in other countries, where important persons are more closely guarded than here.

Quite apart from an attempt at violence, there was the possibility of a demonstration by one or other of the various groups

137

with a grievance aaginst the Marshal's regime; the Italians on account of Trieste, the Communists on account of his breakaway from the Cominform; the Fascists on account of his communism; and the Roman Catholics on account of his treatment of the church and the bishops; not to mention the various Serb and Croat groups who, during and since the war, had been at enmity with Tito, and many of whose members had suffered imprisonment and execution.

Over our heads all the time, as we planned, hung the shadow of Sarajevo and its consequences. As soon as the visit was definitely decided upon, Commander Burt organised a thorough check, with the assistance of chief constables throughout the country, on all possible suspects from the Balkans and Central Europe. They scanned lists of all registered aliens, considering their history and what was known about those who were worth special attention. We were also given a certain number of names by the Yugoslav and our own intelligence services, while the Home Office, through the immigration officers, instituted a strict control on all landings at ports and airports.

At the same time, I considered the steps we ought to take during his visit for the physical protection of Marshal Tito. As in the case of other visiting Heads of States, selected detectives would be attached to him for the duration of his stay and would co-operate with any security officers he might bring with him; but something more than this seemed to be necessary, particularly for the occasions when he would be travelling through the streets or visiting places outside London. The mounted escort which accompanies the Sovereign or visiting Heads of States is picturesque, but it can hardly be said to provide more than a symbolic protection. Taking a leaf out of the American notebook, I decided to give the Marshal an escort of motor-cyclists. The police motor-cycle patrol, by his training and experience, is a rider of superb skill in all conditions, and a team was therefore chosen from among them. Sixteen constables, four drawn from each district, went into training at Hendon and worked out the most suitable formation for this unusual duty. When, on the Marshal's arrival, they went into action, they certainly set everyone talking, for nothing like them had ever been seen in London before.

They escorted the Marshal's car on all his London journeys and enabled him to maintain a punctual time-table throughout a crowded week; while by arrangement with the chief constables concerned, they also accompanied him on his journeys outside the Metropolitan Police District to Windsor and Duxford. We were fortunately able to equip them just in time with the newly approved crash helmets; painted black with a blue band and the Metropolitan Police badge, and by their smart appearance and good riding they demonstrated the ceremonial possibilities of this – for London – novel form of escort, which was later to do excellent service during the Queen's drives through London after the Coronation.

But their function was by no means only of a ceremonial nature. The greatest danger of an attempt on the life of the Marshal was clearly at times when he was standing still or moving slowly within easy reach of a crowd. Carefully planned co-operation between the police on foot and the motor-cycle escort ensured that his car was not held up in any traffic blocks, and the escort was so arranged that two riders could always close up on the car if they should be needed, and could quickly deal with anyone who attempted to run towards it. The car itself was bullet-proof, and it was a tribute to the peacefulness of English political life that no such car was available in this country. The car used was placed at our disposal by the Government of Northern Ireland.

The date of the visit and details of the programme were treated as secret, for obvious reasons, since the earlier they became known, the longer any ill-disposed persons would have to make their plans. The date of the Marshal's arrival was at a fairly late stage put forward from March 23 to 16. Even to the police, the port where he was to disembark was known only a few days beforehand.

As the visit was not a state visit, protocol did not allow the Marshal to stay at Buckingham Palace. The choice of somewhere suitable for him to stay therefore became important. It clearly had to be somewhere which could be well guarded, and for this reason a hotel was out of the question and I pressed strongly for some private residence. Eventually, White Lodge, in Richmond Park, was suggested. From the police point of view this was an admirable choice, since it was reasonably near London, yet stood apart on high ground from which all the approaches to it were visible. Also there was a choice of various routes to and from London.

It was obvious that the place where the Marshal was staying

could not be kept secret for long after his arrival, but until then there was no object in advertising it. During the visit the house was surrounded by an armed police guard, reinforced by police dogs, and kept in touch by telephone and wireless with police headquarters. There were also mobile searchlights to flood-light the grounds in case of trouble.

As soon as the Marshal's programme was available, we drew up detailed plans for policing points where danger might occur, and all the routes to be followed were specially surveyed. In particular, arrangements were made to signal the progress of the Port of London Authority barge *Nore* up the Thames from Greenwich to Westminster Pier, so that the bridges under which it would pass, which were obvious danger spots, could be cleared with the least possible interference with traffic.

As Westminster Pier, where the Marshal was due to land, is overlooked both from Westminster Bridge and the Victoria Embankment, I felt there was a need for special precautions, and police cordons were arranged to keep the bridge and part of the Embankment on either side of the pier clear of people. The pier itself was rigorously examined for explosives by the Port of London Authority Police and Metropolitan officers of 'A' Division, and a guard was put upon it from Saturday night until the Marshal's arrival on Monday afternoon.

While all these precautions were taken, I was concerned to see that every reasonable facility should be given to the representatives of the press, the newsreels and the B.B.C., whose duty it would be to give the world a full and early account of what promised to be a visit of outstanding political importance. Reporters, photographers and radio commentators from Yugoslavia had a special claim to our help, and the B.B.C. emphasised the importance of a full coverage in the broadcasts in various languages to European countries. At the same time, it was important that the Marshal should not be inconvenienced by too many reporters, and I therefore suggested that I should issue special cards to a limited number of approved reporters, photographers and newsreel operators, on the understanding that they would work together on behalf of all the various interests and share the results. This was agreed, and I understand it worked satisfactorily. It certainly eased the task of the police.

As the visit drew near, it was impossible to avoid a feeling of anxiety. I was not surprised, therefore, when, on the preceding Thursday, the Prime Minister asked me to go and see him. Sir Winston Churchill told me that Marshal Tito was unpopular with a number of people, some of whom would not stick at murder. What was I doing for his protection? I outlined for him what steps we had taken. What, he asked, had we done about Westminster Pier? I told him, and he seemed satisfied. Two days later, he asked me to see him at the House of Commons, and again inquired about Westminster Pier. Again I told him what had been arranged.

'I'd like to go and have a look,' he said, and we went out together through the subway from the House on to the Embankment. When we had reconnoitred the ground, he emphasised that it would be wise to keep clear of people all the places from which the pier was overlooked.

On Monday, the morning of the Marshal's arrival, the Prime Minister sent for me a third time, and asked me to go over our arrangements once more. When I had finished, he asked, 'Are you satisfied?'

I said I was.

'Well, of course, it's your responsibility,' he said grimly, and with that consoling thought I returned to Scotland Yard.

There was nothing more to be done but await events and hope for the best. I was present on the pier when the Marshal arrived. He was a cheerful, intelligent-looking man, obviously in the pink of condition, who read his speech in an English to which he was clearly unaccustomed. He did not seem unduly perturbed by any foreboding of disaster.

In fact, the only incident of his visit happened just as his car was moving away from the pier, when somebody in the crowd near Westminster Station threw a smoke-bomb. Nobody saw it thrown, and nobody was arrested. The bomb went off in the gutter, causing a small panic in the neighbourhood, but that was all.

I had regular reports about the Marshal's movements each day, but there was nothing of moment to record. I saw him a second time at a reception given by the Yugoslav Ambassador, when I sampled slivovitz for the first time. (I am willing to try anything once, but not slivovitz again.) On the last morning of his visit, he called in the two detectives who had been attached to him, and presented them with gold cigarette cases, and later I received a letter of thanks from the Yugoslav Ambassador expressing appreciation of all that we had done. On April 1 in the House of Commons the Prime Minister said, 'I do not think it is going too far to state that the whole visit was an unqualified success and has made a contribution of major importance to mutual collaboration and understanding, as well as to the general cause of peace.'

It was a source of great satisfaction to the Metropolitan Police to have played their part in this historic visit, and to know that our distinguished guest had gone home with such pleasant impressions of this country. One would have preferred him to see us with the same informality as other V.I.P.s, but the risks were too great. It was perhaps no bad thing that everyone should realise how quickly and effectively police control can be stepped up to a point hitherto unknown here, if only to demonstrate how necessary it is to maintain a vigilant watch on our liberties, so that the exceptional measures of that week never become the normal.

Since the war we have been little troubled by disorders arising from the activities of political parties, but when they have occurred the burden of dealing with them has mainly fallen, not on the Special Branch, but on the uniformed police. The Fascist movement, which before the war had a considerable following, was sternly dealt with during the war and survived only in a very attenuated form. But as soon as the Fascists were able to renew their agitation they did so, under the name of the Union Movement, and in the most provocative form, organising marches and meetings in those parts of the East End with a predominantly Jewish population. This excited counter-demonstrations and eventually some minor breaches of the peace. When these occurred it seemed to me time to intervene, and having obtained the approval of the Home Secretary, I made an Order on April 29, 1948, under the Public Order Act of 1936, forbidding any political processions in a considerable area of East London. This the Fascists evaded by organising a march immediately outside the prohibited area, as a result of which there was a serious outbreak of disorder and thirty-one people were arrested. I therefore made a new Order on May 6 covering the whole of the Metropolitan Police District. The Act gave me power to do this for a period of three months, and as during that time the Union Movement, though debarred from organising processions, continued to hold meetings in the streets of the East End, at which there were frequent clashes between them and their opponents, I renewed the

Order for a further three months until November 6. By then matters had improved and there had been very little disorder at the meetings, so I decided to let the ban on processions lapse, in the hope that the Union Movement would avoid further provocation.

Regular meetings continued to be held in the Dalston area, and Chief Superintendent Satterthwaite and his officers of 'G' Division spent their week-ends in keeping the contestants apart, or closing the meetings when they threatened to degenerate into a free fight. I saw Satterthwaite regularly and impressed upon him the importance of impartiality, but at the same time told him that he would have my backing if he took strong action where there was a disturbance. Satterthwaite, a downright man, saw the ringleaders of the trouble and left them in no doubt what his instruction were and he was, I believe, grateful for the support I gave him. I need scarcely say that the police, whose leave rosters were being upset, were thoroughly fed up with the whole business, and called down a plague on both Fascist and Communist houses.

The position of the police was an unenviable one, for the Fascists complained that the police had failed to protect them in the exercise of their right of free speech, while the Jews and Communists complained that the Fascists were being protected by the police while they organised grossly provocative and insulting meetings in areas where they were calculated to be most resented. These contradictory complaints were good evidence to me that the police were maintaining an impartial attitude.

After a month or two the Union Party became more active, and eventually organised a new procession at which there was considerable disorder, so the ban was reimposed on March 22, 1949, for three months. This had a rather more lasting effect than the earlier prohibition, and the summer passed fairly peacefully; but in the autumn a march from Mare Street to Ridley Road met with more or less organised opposition from a body of young Jewish Communists known as the Forty-three Group, and it was necessary to make twelve arrests.

It became obvious after a few weeks that if I did not re-impose the ban on processions the disorder would grow worse, for they were attracting not only the political opponents of the Fascists, but also numbers of young hooligans who saw in them a chance of creating a disturbance for its own sake. When a procession was planned for October 4 it was certain that disorder would follow, so I reimposed the ban from October 3 for three months, and except for a brief interval in January, 1950, renewed it every three months until the spring of 1951, when it was due to expire just before May Day.

All the world over May Day is the day when there are Socialist and Communist demonstrations, and in London for many years the London Trades Council had been accustomed to organise a series of orderly processions from the different quarters of London to Trafalgar Square, and there hold a great meeting. In 1950, these processions, which are clearly political in character, had come under the prohibition contained in my Order, and had not taken place. This was resented by those who wished to hold the usual May Day processions, and they suggested that I ought to limit my order to Fascist processions and that if I did not do so, my action was due to class bias. In fact, under the Act I had no power to discriminate. It had to be all or none. But in 1951 I was very anxious not to renew the Order, for three reasons. First, because on general grounds I dislike prohibitions which run counter to our traditional ideas of liberty of speech and action, and had no wish to impose a ban, except in the last resort; second, because the prohibition having been in force continuously for over twelve months, it might be suggested with some show of reason that I was seeking to make permanent what Parliament had expressly said was to be temporary; and third – and from the practical point of view, more important – because I had come to the conclusion that the need had passed and that the ban could safely be lifted without fear of renewed disorder.

Indeed, it seemed to me disorder was more likely to result from an attempt to stop the May Day procession, which had always been orderly in the past, than from any small demonstrations that might be arranged by the divided and disorganised groups of Fascist sympathisers. I decided, therefore, not to reimpose the prohibition. The Union Party had set out to be provocative, and the attempts of their opponents to interfere with their meetings had played into their hands and given them a publicity they would never have achieved by their own efforts. The leaders of the Jewish community, realising this, persuaded the groups opposing the Union Party that it would be better to ignore their meetings. Coupled with the patient and firm handling of the situation by the local police, this has been rewarded by an almost complete absence of disorder for the past two years.

One incident will be long remembered. The Scottish Nationalists had attracted little attention south of the border, and even in Scotland had not over-stepped the bounds of ordinary political agitation, when on Christmas Eve, 1950, they staged a coup which provided a nine days' wonder by stealing the Stone of Scone from the Coronation Chair in Westminster Abbey.

Chapter 15
THE STONE OF SCONE

THE Stone of Scone was brought to England in 1296 by
Edward I after his victory over the Scots. It was built into a
chair by Walter, the King's Painter, and on it the Kings and
Queens of England have been crowned ever since. To the
Scottish Nationalists it was a symbol of Scottish independence,
and a little group formed the idea of seizing the Stone and
conveying it to Scotland in order to draw public attention to
their grievances.

Information had earlier been received by Scotland Yard of
a possible attempt to seize the King's Stone at Kingston-on-
Thames, on which the Saxon Kings had been crowned. Further
information came that a prominent member of the extremist
wing of Scottish Nationalism had left Scotland for England by
car, and for a time police were set to watch the King's Stone
by day and night. No rumour, however, of an attempt on the
Stone of Scone had reached us. The theft of it was carried out
by a party of amateurs, whose efforts were certainly attended
by beginners' luck. Indeed, when they were at last found and
interviewed by the police, they gave a strong impression that
they had no idea they would be successful in removing the
Stone. They had intended to attempt its removal during the
day, when the Abbey was open, and the fact that they would
have been seen and arrested did not seem to interest them
because, they explained, they would have achieved their object
in the publicity which their arrest would have created.

On Christmas Eve, 1950, Westminster Abbey was closed to
the public at five in the evening, and the verger locked the doors
and the iron gates outside the Poets' Corner. Just after nine
o'clock the verger went out into the Cloisters and saw the
Archdeacon talking to two students outside the gate. The
Archdeacon asked him to open the gate and let them in so that
he could show them certain interesting parts of the building.
After about ten minutes the students left. The verger noticed
that they both spoke with a Scottish accent.

At a quarter to eleven the verger handed over to the fireman and the night watchman, who made their usual rounds of inspection during the night and noticed nothing wrong until soon after six in the morning, when the watchman found that the door at Poets' Corner had been forced open. He immediately went to Henry VII's Chapel and made sure that the silver candlesticks and cross at the Battle of Britain Memorial were safe. He then went into Edward the Confessor's Chapel, and found that the Coronation Stone, which weighs about forty-five pounds, was missing.

As soon as the loss was reported to the police, the head of the C.I.D. telephoned me at home and told me what had occurred. He had placed Detective Chief Inspector McGrath of 'A' Division, in whose territory the Abbey stands, in charge of the investigation, and assured me that everything possible was being done to clear the matter up.

When McGrath arrived at the Abbey that morning he found that the gate leading from the roadway at Old Palace Yard to the Poets' Corner was open, and that the wooden doors on the right of the carriageway leading from the gate to the Poets' Corner door had been forced. The bolt and padlock had been wrenched off, and through the door it was possible to enter a yard used by masons working on the Abbey and so reach the Poets' Corner door, which had also been forced from the outside, as was shown by the marks of a jemmy. The screws which had secured the pivot plate for the bolt on the Mason's Yard door were missing. Inside the Abbey McGrath found that the woodwork of the Chair had been damaged in removing the Stone, and under the Chair were a jemmy and a man's wrist-watch. Marks on the floor showed that the Stone had been dragged from the Chair through the door leading to the High Altar, and then down the Altar steps and along the aisle to the Poets' Corner door.

The Chief Inspector at once interviewed all possible witnesses. A young constable without much experience had been on duty outside the Abbey early that morning. He remembered having seen a black Ford Anglia car with no lights parked in the road leading to the Poets' Corner door at about quarter past five that morning. In it were a man and woman who, when asked to explain why they were on private property, replied with a Scottish accent that they were on tour and trying to find somewhere to sleep. The constable directed them to the car park in Great College Street nearby. He described the woman as aged between twenty-two and twenty-five, with long dark hair, dark eyes, a sharp-pointed nose and thin lips, and of a fair complexion. The man was two or three years older, of medium build, with fair, uncombed hair, and a slightly snub nose. The girl had not spoken much, but the man had seemed to want to keep on talking and spoke with a very broad Scots accent. While they were talking there was a loud bang inside the Abbey, at which the young policeman, in the spirit of Christmas, said, 'I expect that's the night watchman falling over.' He shone his torch into the back of the car, but saw only a travelling rug. (Under it, according to the book published later by Ian Hamilton, was a piece of the Stone which had come away while they were removing it.)

The car drove off after a few minutes, and the policeman tested the iron gates at the end of the carriageway, about fifteen yards from the Poets' Corner entrance. He also shone his torch on the Poets' Corner door, but from that distance it seemed secure. He did not notice the wooden doors which had been forced. He saw lights in the Abbey, but decided they were probably caused by someone preparing for the Christmas service, and went on his way.

Next, Inspector McGrath interviewed the verger, who remembered having found a man in the Abbey after it was closed on the evening of December 23. The man was hiding behind a statue in the North Transept and was in his stockinged feet, carrying one shoe in his left hand, the other being in his jacket pocket. He said in a Scottish accent that he had been locked in when the Abbey was closed, and was afraid to call out in case he got into trouble. He gave the name of Allison, and said that he worked as a goods clerk at Paddington Station. Although he could not produce his identity card, the verger accepted his story and let him out of the North Door.

The evidence so far pointed to Scottish Nationalists as the instigators of the theft, and the inquiry was being directed accordingly when, on December 29, a petition to the King was left on the counter of the *Glasgow Herald* office. It read:

The Petition of certain of His Majesty's most loyal and obedient subjects to His Majesty King George VI HUMBLY SHEWETH,

THAT His Majesty's Petitioners are the persons who

148

removed the Stone of Destiny from Westminster Abbey,

THAT in removing the Stone of Destiny they have no desire to injure His Majesty's Property nor to pay disrespect to the Church of which he is temporal head,

THAT the Stone of Destiny is however the most ancient symbol of Scottish nationality and having been removed from Scotland by force and retained in England in breach of the pledge of His Majesty's predecessor King Edward III of England, its proper place of retention is among His Majesty's Scottish people who above all hold this symbol dear.

THAT therefore His Majesty's Petitioners will most readily return the Stone to the safe keeping of His Majesty's officers if His Majesty will but graciously assure them that in all time coming the Stone will remain in Scotland in such of His Majesty's properties or otherwise as shall be deemed fitting by him,

THAT such an assurance will in no way preclude the use of the Stone in any Coronation of any of His Majesty's successors, whether in England or in Scotland,

THAT His Majesty's Humble Petitioners are prepared to submit to His Majesty's Ministers or their representatives proof that they are the people able, willing and eager to restore the Stone of Destiny to the keeping of His Majesty's officers.

THAT His Majesty's Petitioners, who have served His Majesty both in peril and in peace, pledge again their loyalty to him, saving always their right and duty to protest against the actions of His Majesty's Ministers if such actions are contrary to the wishes or the spirit of His Majesty's Scottish people.

IN WITNESS OF the good faith of His Majesty's Petitioners the following additional information concerning a watch left in Westminster Abbey on 25th December, 1950, is appended:

(i) the mainspring of the watch was recently repaired,

(ii) the bar holding the right-hand wrist strap to the watch had recently been broken and soldered.

> This information is given in lieu of signature by His Majesty's Petitioners being in fear of apprehension.

Though the petition was unsigned, the reference to the damaged watch was sufficiently accurate to show that the writers were connected with the raid.

Every day suggestions as to the whereabouts of the Stone poured into Scotland Yard, were examined and, where it seemed worth while, followed up. One writer declared that, given a few facts about the Stone, he would have no difficulty in locating it by some occult process of which he was master, but his offer of help was considered redundant by the C.I.D. The only concrete piece of evidence which turned up was the finding, on January 6, of a plaque with a description of the chair, which usually stood on the seat. This was discovered on a bombed site in Tufton Street, near the Abbey.

As it was obvious that further investigation in London would take us no further, the inquiry moved to Scotland, where Chief Inspector McGrath sought the help of the Glasgow Police. As a result of 'information received', on January 23, they interviewed a Miss Katrine Bell Mathieson, a domestic science teacher. She denied having any knowledge of the theft of the Stone, though she added, 'But if I had I would not tell you.' She said she had spent Christmas at home in Ross-shire. Not being satisfied, the officers made further inquiries and found that she could drive a car and had left her lodgings in Glasgow on December 22 *en route* to London, that she had been seen travelling home by train at Dingwall on December 27, and had telephoned the proprietress of a hotel near her home and asked that a message should be passed on to her mother, reminding her that if the police inquired about her movements at Christmas, her mother was to be sure to say that she arrived home on December 25. It was later learned that when the police had left her after this interview, she again telephoned the hotel proprietress and asked her to deliver an urgent message to her mother to the same effect.

On the evening of January 30, a notice was found on the steps of St Giles's Cathedral, Edinburgh. It said:

We, the persons who removed the Stone of Destiny from Westminster Abbey on Christmas morning, 1950, and who brought it over the border on Hogmanay, 1950, wish to make the following pronouncement to the Scottish people and to ask their instructions regarding the disposal of the Stone.

In face of imprisonment we reaffirm our resolution to

retain this ancient symbol of Scottish nationality in our country unless it be the clearly demonstrated will of the Scottish people that the Stone be handed back to the Church of England.

We therefore suggest that the next meeting of the Scottish National Assembly decide the future resting-place of the Stone, and we solemnly bind ourselves to abide by any decision that this Assembly may take, for we are convinced that the Assembly is the only body capable of expressing the will of the people of Scotland. Should it be the decision of the Assembly that the Stone be returned to England we shall relinquish it to whatever agents the English Church may appoint or otherwise as the Assembly may deem fitting. If on the other hand the Assembly decide that the Stone shall remain in Scotland, it is our earnest hope that the Assembly shall treat with the London authorities to the purpose that the Stone may find its permanent resting-place not in the shrine of a people who value it as one of the spoils of war but in the capital of a nation who would proudly regard it as the symbol of their liberty.

In proof of our good faith we issue the following information not yet released by the Police:

(1) On the night of Saturday, 23rd December, 1950, one of our number was ejected from Westminster Abbey by the watchman half an hour after the Abbey had closed. Our associate's name was John Allison of Arlington Street, N.14.

(2) The nail with which this document is affixed to the door of St Giles's Cathedral was recently removed from the fabric of Westminster Abbey.

It was in fact a screw that was left on the steps of the Cathedral, and McGrath was satisfied that it was one of those wrenched off the Masons' Yard gate at the Abbey.

On March 16, Miss Matheson's mother was seen and duly confirmed that her daughter had arrived home on the evening of Christmas Day. But when the police interviewed Miss Matheson again she realised her story would no longer stand up, and agreed to make a statement. It is perhaps symptomatic of the state of tension in which these young people were on the night of the theft that Miss Matheson believed that she, not the policeman, had made the remark about the watchman falling

151

down; and when her companions were later interviewed, there were minor discrepancies between their statements which could be accounted for by a very natural state of nerves during their exploit. After Miss Matheson had made her statement, she added that she had intended to speak only in Gaelic, but for some unknown reason had changed her mind. She refused to reveal the names of her companions.

Meanwhile, however, inquiries at garages in and near Glasgow showed that a Ford Anglia car had been hired in Glasgow on December 22 by Gavin Vernon, a student, aged twenty-four, and returned on December 29, having travelled 1,479 miles. Shortly before this, another student named Ian Hamilton, aged twenty-five, had inquired of the same garage about the hire of a car, but the garage had declined to do business with him, so he went away, but returned later with Vernon, to whom the car was hired.

Then it occurred to a Glasgow policeman to inquire at the City Library whether anyone had recently borrowed books on Westminster Abbey, and the record showed that three such books had been issued to Hamilton on September 29, 1950. Further inquiry indicated a third man, Alexander Stuart, aged twenty, as having been concerned in the affair, and he, Vernon and Hamilton were all seen and interrogated. Hamilton denied any part in the theft and declined to make a statement, but Inspector McGrath observed that he seemed to enjoy it when the Inspector gave him an opportunity of explaining whom he considered should be the lawful custodian of the Stone. Stuart and Vernon did make statements, but neither would give the names of their accomplices. From their accounts and that of Miss Matheson, the story of the theft can be reconstructed.

Vernon and three friends decided just before Christmas to go to the Abbey and steal – or, as they preferred to put it, recover – the Stone of Scone. Vernon hired a Ford Anglia car, and on the evening of Friday, December 22, set off with Hamilton for London, accompanied by Stuart and Miss Matheson in a similar car belonging to Stuart's father. They arrived in London the following afternoon and drove around for a time to see the town. Later, Hamilton went to the Abbey with the intention of remaining inside after it was closed in order to see what went on; but soon afterwards he rejoined his companions having been turned out of the Abbey by the verger, to whom he had given the name of Allison.

152

That night all four slept in their cars, and the next afternoon visited the Abbey to reconnoitre the ground. They decided that the door in the Poets' Corner was the easiest way to get into the Abbey, and duly noted the wooden gates to the Masons' Yard. Later that evening, Vernon and Stuart walked round Dean's Yard and there occurred the meeting with the Archdeacon. All four again returned to their cars to sleep, intending to take the Stone on the Monday morning when the Abbey was open; but they woke up cold, and decided to act straightaway.

They had already prepared their entrance by forcing the bar off the wooden door into the Masons' Yard, and Vernon related how he had put the four screws from the plate into his pocket and later into the cubby-hole of one of the cars.

They drove the two cars to the car park in Great College Street, and leaving Vernon's car there, were all driven back to the Abbey, by Miss Matheson. She reversed the car up the road to Poets' Corner and the three men went in, forced open the Poets' Corner door with a jemmy, entered the Abbey and took the Stone from the Coronation Chair. They found it much heavier than they had expected, so they put it in Hamilton's coat and dragged it through the Sanctuary to the Poets' Corner door. At this point they heard the car outside start up, and hurriedly sent Hamilton out to tell Miss Matheson to stop it. Miss Matheson had seen a policeman moving across the road towards her, and in an effort to divert his attention from the Abbey, had moved the car forward in the roadway. Hamilton hastily jumped into the car, and together they told the constable that they were tourists looking for a place to sleep.

Vernon and Stuart, unaware of what was happening outside, carried the Stone across the Masons' Yard to the wooden gates and, peeping through the keyhole, saw the policeman beside the car and heard his remark about the watchman falling down. Miss Matheson and Hamilton then drove off without being able to communicate with their companions, and on Hamilton's instructions Miss Matheson set off alone for Scotland.

After the policeman had gone, Vernon and Stuart went to the car park to fetch their car. Just before they got there, they saw a police van drive by and, fearing the alarm had been given, decided to collect the car and drive off at once. When they got to Great College Street, however, they could not find the car key. Now thoroughly scared, they walked away and after some time, by pure chance, met Hamilton driving the car

153

they had gone to fetch.

Hamilton, having seen Miss Matheson safely away, had returned to the Great College Street car park. On reaching it, he also had realised that he had not got the key, but he remembered it had been in the pocket of his overcoat, which had been used to drag the Stone away, so he had gone back again into the Abbey, and by good luck found the key on the floor. He had then collected the car from the car park, returned a third time to the Abbey, and put the Stone in the back of the car under his overcoat. He had been driving blindly about London, lost in a maze of streets, when he chanced to see Vernon and Stuart walking along. It was then agreed that Vernon should return to Glasgow by train, and Stuart and Hamilton should drive the car away. Vernon returned to Glasgow and later met his two companions, who handed the car over to him. He returned it to the garage.

The other two drove down into Kent and shortly before reaching Rochester, hid the Stone in a wood near the road. They then drove off to Scotland, where the Stone was taken later on. The plaque that had been on the chair was thrown away on the bombed site in Tufton Street, where it was afterwards found. The petition left at the *Glasgow Herald* office and the notice found on the door of St Giles's Cathedral were both written by Stuart and Hamilton.

The impression one gains from the book written by Hamilton about this exploit is that it was a student's escapade, motivated by an almost religious fire. Hamilton, who declares that he was the man in the car seen by the policeman and also the one found in the Abbey the night before the theft, seems to have had a great animus against England, with little knowledge of it, and regarded himself as a crusader on behalf of an oppressed country. If his book is to be believed, he was given encouragement by elderly Scottish Nationalists who might have been expected to know better.

So much for the theft of the Stone. Now for its return. The police in their search for the Stone had dragged the Serpentine and other likely stretches of water in and about London where it might be expected to have been hidden. Then the search shifted to Scotland where we were pretty certain it had been taken. We still had no idea where it was, however, until on April 11, 1951, a school teacher, Mr David Alistair Gardner of Arbroath, a town councillor and member of the Scottish

Nationalist Party, went to Arbroath police station and reported that the Stone was on the High Altar in the ruined Abbey of Arbroath.

According to the stories of Mr Gardner and of Mr Frank Thornton, an outfitter, also an Arbroath councillor and Scottish Nationalist, they were asked some time before April 11 to act as intermediaries for the return of the Stone. They would not disclose the names of the persons for whom they were acting, and from Mr Gardner's description of them, the men who returned the Stone were not the three who had taken it, but were much older.

About midday on April 11, Mr Thornton went to Arbroath Abbey and a car with three men drew up. The Stone was taken from the boot, carried on a stretcher under the flag of St Andrew into the Abbey, and placed on the High Altar. Mr Wishart, Custodian of the Abbey, remembered having seen Mr Gardner standing outside the office at this time, but as he was busy selling postcards to sightseers, asked him to wait. When he had finished selling postcards, he said to Mr Gardner, 'Is that the Stone of Destiny?'

Mr Gardner replied, 'Yes, that is the Stone of Destiny. It is being handed over.'

Mr Wishart then said, 'They should have asked my permission before coming in here with that Stone, because I am in charge here.'

He had, however, accepted custody of the Stone, and as the men who had brought it left, one of them said to him, 'I am very pleased to have met you and to have given you the honour of accepting the Stone of Destiny.' Mr Wishart knew none of them.

Two sealed envelopes addressed to His Majesty the King and the General Assembly of the Church of Scotland were placed on the Stone. A copy of the letter to the King was sent by the writers to the newspapers. It read:

Unto His Majesty King George VI, the Address of His Majesty's Scottish subjects who removed the Stone of Destiny from Westminster Abbey and have since retained it in Scotland.

Humbly sheweth ... that in their actions they, as loyal subjects, have intended no indignity or injury to His Majesty or to the Royal Family.

They have been inspired in all they have done by their deep love of His Majesty's Realm of Scotland and by their desire to compel the attention of His Majesty's Ministers to the widely expressed demand of Scottish people for a measure of self government.

The police recovered the Stone from Arbroath Abbey and removed it to Forfar Police Station. The next day it was taken to Glasgow Central Police Station, where the Clerk of Works at Westminster Abbey examined and identified it. The Stone had been slightly damaged at one corner, but the damage had been repaired and otherwise it was intact. The following day the Stone was taken by road to London, where soon after eight o'clock in the evening, in the presence of the Home Secretary, it was handed over to the Dean in the Abbey.

The Stone having been recovered, it only remained to decide whether proceedings should be taken against those responsible for its removal. On April 19, the Attorney-General, Sir Hartley Shawcross, announced his decision in the House of Commons in answer to a question by Mr Henderson Stewart.

'The police,' he said, 'conducted very full and, if I may say so, very able inquiries into this deplorable affair and I have now considered their report. The report included statements by three out of the four persons who are believed to have been concerned in removing the Stone from Westminster Abbey, in which each admitted the part he himself had played, but did not implicate the others, or indicate the then whereabouts of the Stone. The clandestine removal of the Stone from Westminster Abbey, the manner of its taking and manifest disregard for the sanctity of the Abbey were vulgar acts of vandalism which have caused great distress and offence both in England and Scotland and have brought the individuals concerned in them into great disrepute. I do not think, however, that the public interest requires that I should direct criminal proceedings to be taken.'

There was a curious little postscript to this affair. On May 16, Ian Hamilton, who had twice denied having had any connection with the theft of the Stone, called at Cannon Row Police Station and asked to see Inspector McGrath. He said that since he had last seen the Inspector in Scotland, he had consulted his engagement book and observed that he had been in Westminster Abbey on Christmas morning and had assisted in removing the Coronation Stone. The watch found in the Abbey was his, and he would like it back.

The Inspector pointed out to him that if he were indeed the owner of the watch, certain formalities had to be completed before it could be returned. Hamilton said he would think about this, and left. He did not call again.

Chapter 16
THE THAMES DIVISION

DURING my Commissionership, I used to go whenever I could in one of the launches of the Thames Division. The river is one of the great sights of London, and it is a pity it is not used more. We would cruise from Battersea Park past the great Palaces of Lambeth and Westminster, past the wonderful view of Waterloo Bridge with St Paul's in the background, the old Customs House and the grey mass of the Tower, into the Pool of London, with its movement of vessels up and down on the tide. Further down, past the docks, is what I think the finest view on the Thames, the river front of Wren's Greenwich Hospital.

John Burns described the Thames as liquid history, and it is appropriate that the Thames police should be older by some thirty years than the Metropolitan Police, of which they now form a Division. They owe their origins to Patrick Colquhoun, a Doctor of Law and a Scot from Dumbarton, who, after serving as Lord Provost of Glasgow, came to London with his family in 1789. He became a magistrate at the Queen's Street Stipendiary Court and devoted much time to a study of the crime which flourished in the London of that day. He wrote a number of books, in which he suggested that the remedy was to be found in a well-organised civilian police force. One of his publications, *A Treatise on the Commerce and Police of the River Thames,* attracted the attention of the West India merchants who were suffering heavy losses from river thieves acting in collusion with ship's crews.

Colquhoun's inquiries showed that something like half the cargoes brought into the Thames failed to reach the warehouses of the merchants. Their own efforts to establish an effective protection society having failed, the merchants invited Colquhoun to form a new River Police. He opened an office at Wapping on the site of the present police station, and with the aid of Captain John Harriott, who was appointed the first magistrate of the new Thames Police Office, set to work to recruit and organise a body of Thames police composed of seamen and watermen. Working in long-oared gigs and armed with blunderbusses and cutlasses, the new police quickly broke up the highly specialised gangs with their romantic-sounding names. The 'Heavy Horsemen', who were dock labourers, concealed stolen goods in their voluminuous clothes, while the 'Light Horsemen', mates of the West Indiamen, augmented by various illicit means their traditional 'perks' of sweepings from the cargoes. 'Game Watermen' and 'Game Lightermen', 'Copemen', 'Long Apron Men', 'Scuffle Hunters' and 'Mud Larks', all preyed happily on the cargoes in their various ways.

The success of the new police, and the need for them, is well illustrated by the story of the river police officer who was employed to watch a ship which was being resheathed with copper. The shipowners ordered ten bags of copper nails and 1,600 sheets of copper, the amount used for the same work on a previous occasion. Yet when the resheathing was complete there was a surplus of three bags of nails and 113 sheets of copper, valued at £71 17s. 4d. Such achievements of the river police greatly helped the passage of Peel's Bill to establish the Metropolitan Police in 1829, and ten years later the Thames Police became a division of the new force. Since then they have carried on their day and night patrol of the Thames, covering a distance which now stretches thirty-six miles from Dartford to Teddington.

The old row boats were replaced by steam launches in 1885, and these in turn gave place to motor boats about 1912. In 1940, the first boat powered by a Diesel engine came into service, and since the war the entire fleet has been replaced by boats of this type. In addition, Diesel patrol launches have been added for the use of the Chief Superintendent and Chief Inspectors. These were originally air-sea rescue launches belonging to the R.A.F., which have been modified to fit them for police work and are capable of speeds up to twenty-four knots.

Since the war, all the boats have been fitted with wireless telephony and are in constant touch with the Information Room at Scotland Yard, so that they can quickly be directed to any part of the river. They also carry a variety of equipment, such as a resuscitator for artificial respiration, stretchers for carrying people who have been injured, various types of dragging gear and salvage materials, pistol rocket line-throwing gear and Aldis lamps for signalling at night. The maintenance and repair of the police boats is all carried out at the workshops at Wapping police station, where there is an up-to-date engineering and shipwright's workshop to which a floating dock was added in 1946.

In addition to their preventive work on the Thames, the river police perform many other duties. Every year they rescue about fifty people from drowning, and secure between one hundred and two hundred drifting barges which, if left to themselves, would cause damage to ships and riverside installations, and salvage thousands of feet of floating timber. They keep a constant watch on those parts of the shore where children come to play, and regularly visit the riverside schools to warn children of dangers to be avoided along the river banks. Nothing, perhaps, has given more pleasure to the men of the river police than the knowledge that as a result of these talks the number of casualties has been greatly reduced in the last few years.

They are, of course, much in evidence at the University boat race. One year, river steamers following the race three abreast caused such a wash, while the banks at Putney were lined with children, that steps had to be taken to limit the number of steamers in future. Another year, Oxford complained that the Commissioner's launch had been so near them as to interfere with their progress. This was not, I hope, a veiled suggestion of sabotage against a Cambridge Commissioner, and in any case I had been well behind the umpires' and the B.B.C. launches.

The River Police make a number of arrests on their own account, but also are often called on to help the police on shore in inquiries which lead to the river and other inland waters. When a search had to be made in ponds or canals, there was always trouble in transporting heavy boats and equipment overland. To overcome this, a flat-bottomed boat, fourteen feet three inches long and with a beam of five feet nine inches was constructed, which is light enough to be readily handled by a crew of three men and can be loaded on to an ordinary police tender and driven wherever it is needed. With a crew and full equipment aboard, it has a draught of only four inches, and rigorous tests have failed to capsize it.

The boat's equipment consists of permanent magnets for recovering iron or steel objects, steel drags to deal with bodies or articles enclosed in sacks, underwater grapnels to locate such things as safes or silverware, a sectional pole drag fitted with a grapnel for lifting articles from the water, and two small anchors to moor the boat fore and aft and keep it steady during a search. This small boat has proved extremely useful. One of its most successful journeys led to the location of a motor car which had been driven into a disused gravel pit with about eighty feet of water in it. The car was found by the boat's magnets, wires were passed underneath it, and it was hauled out of the water by a bulldozer. The car owner, who had reported it as stolen, did not seem as pleased to recover his car as he might have been. It was afterwards found that he had paid for the car to be done away with, and had claimed the insurance on it. He was charged, and sentenced to nine months' imprisonment.

On the river, too, the magnets have been very useful. When, for example, a Polish soldier was found shot on Westminster Bridge in 1945, the river police searched the river-bed below for many days with the magnets. They collected between two and three hundredweights of metal objects, including some safes, nuts, bolts, a car starting-handle, and three revolvers, one of which was later identified as that from which the fatal shots had been fired.

Like the land divisions, the river police have the help of a band of Special Constables, mostly sailors or yachtsmen who love the river and boats. They do regular tours of duty, and every year at Christmas-time turn out in special strength to patrol the river so as to let their regular colleagues enjoy Christmas dinner at home.

In 1952, the Lords Commissioners of the Admiralty granted all police boats authority to fly the Blue Ensign 'defaced' with the badge of the Metropolitan Police. This recognition by the senior service of the part played by the Thames Division in making the river safe for all who have their business on its water, has been received with pleasure and pride by all river policemen past and present.

Chapter 17
THE WOMEN POLICE

THE London policewoman has become such a familiar sight in recent years that it is hard to realise that 1919 it was legally impossible for them to join the Force for, as in most professions, a woman was debarred merely by reason of her sex. Through the years of agitation for women's suffrage many of the most progressive women of their day were at open warfare with the police, and presented them with what must have been one of the most distasteful tasks they ever faced.

There was, however, one very early pioneer of women police, for in 1907 Miss Macdougal was attached to the Criminal Investigation Department to take statements from, and make arrangements for the welfare of, girl victims of sexual offences who might be in danger of being drawn into prostitution. Miss Macdougal was not attested as a policewoman and had no police powers. She worked alone, and in spite of a recommendation by a departmental committee in 1913 in favour of the appointment of women police officers in all large towns, opinion continued to be sceptical of, and even hostile to, the idea.

It was the social problems of the first world war that provided the opportunity for women to demonstrate their value, and though they could not be attested as constables, many hundreds did good service in the Voluntary Patrols and the Women Police Service which operated in and around the great munition factories and hostels. In 1917, the Commissioner of Police formed a body of one hundred women patrols and twelve sergeants for welfare work in London among women and children. The passing of the Sex Disqualification Removal Act in 1919 lifted the legal barrier to their enrolment as regular constables, but the Geddes economy measures which followed the war dealt an almost mortal blow, and in 1922 their numbers were reduced to twenty.

Two years later they were raised to fifty, and advantage was taken of the new Act to swear them as regular constables. In 1934, the establishment was raised to 200, but fewer than this had been enrolled when war broke out. The success of women in the Services and many other spheres during the war removed the last doubts, and when immediately after the war I proposed increasing the strength of the Women Police in London to 300, the suggestion received the immediate approval of the Home Secretary. Since then the numbers have been increased still further and there are now over 450 women police in the Metropolitan Police District.

It was easy enough in 1945 to increase their establishment, but if we were to recruit the right type of woman quickly, there were still some obstacles to be got over. The first was that of dress. The old-fashioned uniform with its helmet and boots was ugly and unlikely to attract anything except ribald criticism. For the women it was neither comfortable nor becoming. The various women's services had evolved during the war quite attractive uniforms, and it was not difficult to devise on similar lines a suitable uniform for the women police. The hat presented a more difficult problem. Various models were produced, including an extraordinary hat resembling the old shako, which did not meet with approval. Fashion parades were attended by the Home Secretary, Mr Chuter Ede, and eventually a cap based on that worn in the Canadian Women's Air Force was chosen. With the blue dress, it is generally agreed to make one of the most attractive women's uniforms now worn.

The second handicap was the limited scope of duties assigned to women. They tended to be concentrated on sexual crime, and while the work was very necessary, and so far as women and girls are concerned could best be done by policewomen, there was an obvious need to widen the field of their work so as to offer an interesting and worth-while career. Consequently the range of the policewomen's duties has been steadily widened since the war, and it is no uncommon thing nowadays for a policewoman to bring in a male prisoner single-handed. More than one rough customer has been surprised, when he showed signs of resistance, to find how firmly he was handled.

In recent years, too, there has been a steady increase in the number of policewomen employed in the Criminal Investigation Department. They are selected, like the men, from the uniform branch after two years' service, and are under the supervision of a Woman Chief Inspector who works at Scotland Yard under the Assistant Commissioner (Crime). Like the uniformed women, they are employed throughout divisions all

163

over London and carry out a wide variety of detective duties. In plain clothes they are specially valuable in observation of various kinds. Not being recognisable as police officers, they are able to enter places where the laws about gaming or drinking are being broken and so secure direct evidence which it would otherwise be almost impossible to get.

A very important problem was that of the relationship between the women police and their male colleagues, by whom they were for a long time regarded with suspicion. The police-man saw in his female counterpart a possible competitor in the labour market who might be used, on grounds of cheap-ness, to undermine his status. The Police Federation steadily declined to admit policewomen to membership, and their atti-tude tended to be reflected in that of the men in the divisions and stations. This situation did not long survive the war. Increased numbers made it possible to post women to almost every station throughout the District, so that more and more men were able to learn from personal knowledge the value of the policewoman's services, while the chronic shortage of men was an incentive to use them as much as possible. As a result, the old hostility and suspicion have disappeared. Women have been admitted as members of the Federation and the Athletic Association, and are fully accepted as a valuable and integral part of the Force. When the Federation nominated a woman sergeant as one of the representatives to argue their claim for improved pay before Sir Trustram Eve in 1951, the women police could safely be said to have arrived. They have indeed come to stay, and it is hard to understand how the police force did without them for so long.

The woman recruit undergoes her initial three months' training alongside the men at Peel House and Hendon, and like the men, is on probation for the rest of her first two years' service. She is subject to the same regulations as to service, discipline and pension, and has the same status, powers and duties. The only differences are that the rate of pay is about ninety per cent. of the men's; she has a shorter working day, when on patrol duty, of seven hours and a half instead of eight; and special provisions are made about marriage and mater-nity.

Soon after the war the rule about resignation on marriage was withdrawn, and quite a number of policewomen continue to serve after marriage, though when, as often happens, the husband is a policeman, conflicting hours of duty can produce a problem. Wherever possible, tours of duty are adjusted sympathetically to meet this difficulty, for we do not want to lose the services of a trained policewoman unnecessarily. Marriage is, in fact, the greatest occupational hazard of the policewoman. In 1952, we lost about fifty women by marriage, and it says much for the attractions of the job that despite this loss there has never been any difficulty in recruiting women quickly whenever the establishment has been raised.

The ranks are the same as those of the men: Constable, Sergeant, Inspector, Chief Inspector, Superintendent and Chief Superintendent.

Shortly after the war, Miss Peto, who had been in charge of the women police since 1934, retired on reaching the age limit. Under her they had come through the difficult years before and during the war with credit and greatly increased experience, and it is on the foundations so well laid by her that the modern force has been built. The question of a successor was a difficult one. After a careful review of those women already in the service, whether in London or the provinces, I was satisfied that to obtain the right type of leader I must go outside the Force, and after interviewing a number of candidates from the Services, as well as from teaching and other professions, we chose Group Officer Elizabeth Bather, O.B.E., of the W.A.A.F.

One of the most important parts of the Chief Superintendent's work is the administration of the Children and Young Persons Acts of 1933 and 1938. She keeps a central index of juveniles, and especially of girls who have come to the notice of the police, and works in close touch with the juvenile courts, probation officers, children's officers, education officers, and the many voluntary organisations concerned with child welfare and the prevention of delinquency.

She is also responsible for arranging courses of two weeks' instruction for young policewomen after they have gained sufficient experience to benefit by them. These courses aim, by lectures and discussion, to widen the students' knowledge of juvenile courts, probation and the after care of women prisoners and Borstal girls, and by personal visits to women's prisons, Borstal Institutions and Approved Schools to let them see at first-hand the conditions and methods of treatment to which offenders are subject after sentence.

As with the men, the basis of the policewoman's work is patrol duty in uniform. The nature of the duty varies according to the part of London where she works. In the West End, police-women patrol the streets, especially around cafés, public houses, amusement centres and railway stations, for these provide the greatest opportunities of watching over the welfare of women and children. Prostitution is one of the chief problems in this area, and the women police play an important part in dealing with it. They not only arrest prostitutes found soliciting in the streets, but are specially charged with the rescue of young girls who have come to the West End from the provinces or the suburbs of London, and are in danger of entering on a life of prostitution.

In the outer suburbs they are employed in patrolling parks and open spaces, where their presence is a deterrent to indecency and assaults on women and children. In the East End and the dock areas they patrol in the streets, and pay special attention to the cafés and other places frequented by coloured seamen which are a haunt of prostitutes.

They keep in close touch with lodging-houses and emergency hostels, and are always on the look-out for girls who may be homeless and in need of accommodation. This patrol duty, linked with a wise use of the juvenile index kept at Scotland Yard, is the means of finding and helping many missing boys and girls.

Policewomen have the same powers of arrest as policemen, and although they do not carry a truncheon and usually get the help of a policeman to arrest a man, they do not hesitate to act alone when they have to. They are trained in self-defence and are quite capable of looking after themselves. Some risk is inevitable in police work, but this is accepted by police-women and there have been many examples of great courage in recent years. The outstanding case occurred when, in order to catch a man who had on several occasions assaulted and robbed women on an unfrequented common in South London, a policewoman, Sergeant Alberta Law, C.I.D., volunteered to act as a decoy in plain clothes. She was attacked and struck on the head with a bottle, but held on to her assailant until help arrived and he was arrested. For her work on this occasion she was awarded the first King's Police Medal for Gallantry to be gained by a woman.

Chapter 18
THE MOUNTED POLICE AND THE DOGS

MY wife was walking home one day through the quiet back streets of Westminster when, herself unnoticed, she saw a mounted policeman who had stopped his horse before a plate-glass shop window. In front of this improvised mirror he was quietly putting his mount through its paces. She spoke to him, and he said, 'I don't often get a chance to see what the horse is doing. I usually put him through it when I come down here and there's nobody about.'

This story symbolises for me the pride the Mounted Branch take in their horses, the constant care to achieve perfection, which would make it a sad day for Londoners if ever the police horse disappeared completely from the City streets.

The Mounted Branch are, like the River Police, an older foundation than the Metropolitan Force itself, for they trace their beginnings back to the Bow Street Horse Patrol of ten men established by the Chief Magistrate, Sir John Fielding, in 1763. Discontinued after a few years on grounds of economy, they were re-established in 1805 and eventually reached a strength of seventy-two men. Their duty was to patrol the main roads leading out of London to a distance of sixteen miles from Charing Cross. Even when the Metropolitan Police Force was established, they remained independent for a time, but in 1839 were incorporated into it.

The horses belonging to the Mounted Branch are bought by the Commissioner, when they are still quite young, generally 'off the grass, from breeders in Yorkshire. The horses chosen are as far as possible all of the same pattern, compact and not under 15.3 hands or over 16.1, since it has been found that the big horse is at a disadvantage manoeuvring in the crowded streets of London.

When a batch of remounts arrives at Imber Court, the head-quarters and training centre of the branch, it requires the eye of an experienced judge to see in many of them, rough and un-schooled as they are, the makings of a future police horse; but care and good feeding, coupled with skilful training, work wonders in two or three months. They are of all colours, but it is traditional for the Commissioner to ride a grey on ceremonial occasions. Winston, the chestnut ridden by both King George VI and Queen Elizabeth II at the ceremony of Trooping the Colour, has achieved great fame, for he appears on the obverse of the crown pieces struck for the Coronation, and on the Great Seal.

The men of the Mounted Branch enter the Force in the ordinary way and pass through the usual training and probation as foot constables. At one time, most of them came from mounted regiments, but with the disappearance of the horse from the army, this source has dried up. So the modern man has to start from scratch, but after six months at Imber Court he becomes an excellent horseman, well up to the high standard of the Branch. After their training, the newcomers are attached to a division as uniform strappers; that is, men fully equipped and trained but without horses. In each division there will be six or more mounted men, and the strapper is therefore able to ride their horses in turn on the days when they are on leave, so keeping up the effective strength on the streets and giving the beginner a variety of rides every week. The daily patrol lasts three hours and a half, and covers some eight miles. Once a man gets his own horse, he may keep him for years and the two become closely attached to each other.

The young horse arriving at Imber Court is allotted to one of the staff and undergoes an intensive course lasting six months. After the horse's confidence has been gained, he is driven for a time on the long rein. Only when he is fully accustomed and obedient to the voice and understands the control of hand and leg conveyed by the long rein, and has been trained to walk, trot, canter and jump, is he mounted for the first time. From then on he goes through a system of schooling designed to make him familiar with, and even contemptuous of, any and every surprise that the streets of London may provide. Flags and rattles, motor cars that backfire or 'rev up', fire, smoke and fire appliances, loading and unloading of vehicles, firearms, and dummies to represent a crowd — everything is presented to the horse in turn. He must learn to go up and down stairs, through fire and water, past fluttering newspapers and dummies that appear suddenly from below or behind trees. The young horse meets in the school all and more than he is ever likely to meet in the street.

After this, he is taught to play push-ball, so that he will know how to shove hard in a crowd. Then follows more jumping, a spell of tent-pegging, and sword, lance and revolver exercises. At the end of all this he emerges as the well-trained police horse, dependable in all circumstances. The best tribute to his training is the complete trust shown by a London crowd when a police horse is in action near them, a trust well-placed, for it is a very rare thing for a police horse to misbehave.

I was taking Norton out one morning at Imber Court when, as we emerged from the paddock, we ran unexpectedly into the shooting of a film which was being made on the training of a police horse. As I drew near, pandemonium broke loose – flags, rattles, revolver shots and the rest all started up. I wondered for a moment how Norton would take it, but I need have had no misgivings. He took no notice whatever.

A horse's useful life varies. He is taken into the Force at three, four or five years, and many are still doing good service after twenty years or even more. They are named on an alphabetical system. All horses bought in 1946 have names beginning with 'A' – Alamein, Alma, Angela (the grey mare I rode in the Coronation procession); in 1947, names beginning with 'B' – Bernadotte, Blenheim; in 1948, Clara; the beautiful little brown mare that won the cup at the Royal Horse Show, Richmond, for the best-trained police horse, and so on. We can at once tell by a horse's name his length of service.

The mounted police are far from being merely a decorative appendage to the regular Force. When, in 1928, the Thames overflowed and parts of Westminster were flooded, mounted police were able to get through the water and rescue the inhabitants of some of the flooded basements. And a mounted officer once made a spectacular rescue in Hyde Park. A small boy was riding with his father in Rotten Row when his pony bolted and galloped away into the fast-moving traffic in East Carriage Road. P.C. Dolman, who was on patrol, saw what was happening and galloped after the pony. As he overtook it, he leaned over and lifted the boy bodily out of the saddle, thus averting what might have been a fatal accident. When I complimented him on his horsemanship he dismissed it as 'all in the day's work'.

The police horse really comes into his own, however, on the occasions when great crowds assemble. The man in the saddle, with his polished leather and glittering metalwork, has an influence over crowds which the foot policeman can rarely equal. When the crowd invaded the pitch at the first Wembley Cup Final in 1923, a single policeman on a grey horse was sufficient to produce order where the foot police had failed.

My first impression of London when I visited it as a boy in 1903, was the steady clip-clop of horses' feet on the wood-paving of the streets. Today, the wood-paving is fortunately fast disappearing, and the motor car has driven the horse out of London; but the police horse remains, and I hope will always remain, a useful and picturesque feature of the London scene.

He has been joined in recent years by another animal ally of the police. One of the most difficult tasks that faced the rescue squads during the blitz was the location of people buried under the debris of bombed houses and buildings. Speed was essential if they were to be rescued before dying of suffocation or pressure of the material on top of them. We experimented with elaborate electrical devices; but in the end, well-trained dogs proved far more effective in this work. Again, in the protection of aerodromes and aircraft factories, trained dogs proved themselves a valuable addition to sentries and watchmen.

With this experience in mind, I was greatly impressed during a visit to Germany in January, 1946, and a later visit to Holland, by the use made in these countries of police dogs. In London there had never been any general use of dogs, although before the war, police officers had been encouraged, by the grant of a small allowance, to keep a dog which could accompany them on their night patrols in the more rural areas. These dogs had no regular training, and were merely the pets of their owners.

On the advice of a Home Office Committee appointed in 1935, arrangements were made for training a small number of dogs, and some provincial Forces took over one or more dogs, mostly Labradors. Two dogs were sent for training by the Metropolitan Police and were employed by the Crime Squad in South London from the middle of 1938 until the outbreak of war. Though they had some success, police officers remained sceptical about their value, and on the outbreak of war they were handed over to the Cheshire Constabulary.

Faced by the record crime figures of 1945, and the probability that our shortage of men would continue for some years,

I decided that it would be well worth while to experiment again with police dogs, even though most of the Metropolitan Police District, being closely built-up, was perhaps not ideal for the purpose. We started in a small way with six Labradors which were trained for work in the outer suburbs. Each dog was always to work with the same handler and live with him in his home.

From the first, we decided that there must be no question of the dogs being allowed to attack offenders, for the scheme would be unlikely to survive long if a dog attacked and seriously injured anyone, whether a criminal or an innocent person. To make an arrest, the dog is trained to seize the offender's right coat-sleeve and hang on at all costs, even if firearms are used, until the handler can come up and make an arrest.

A training centre with kennels was established temporarily at Imber Court, but has lately been transferred to more suitable quarters at West Wickham. Here, new dogs and their handlers undergo three months' training before they go out on police duty. They return at intervals for refresher training, since work in city streets, with their confused noises and smells, tends to blunt the dogs' sensibilities. The dog is first taught complete obedience to his handler, and continues with tracking, searching an area or buildings for a person or for missing articles, and the arrest of someone trying to escape. The supersonic whistle, audible to dogs but not to human beings, enables a handler to control his dog while watching suspects, without their being aware that they are being watched. Very often the mere presence of the dog is enough to make a person come quietly, but whether he does so or not, there is no instance of a dog losing his man once he has taken charge. One dog, Ben, a Labrador, developed a technique of his own. Instead of seizing the sleeve, he found it as effective to run between the offender's legs and trip him up.

Labradors were the first dogs to be employed, but after a time a trial was given to Alsatians, and they are now in the majority. Among many people they have a bad name for unreliability, but this is not confirmed by our experience, and their strength, speed and intelligence fit them admirably for police purposes.

In the early days of this experiment, the dogs were used mainly to accompany officers on their rounds in the suburbs where there were open spaces or detached houses standing in their own grounds. Here the keen senses of the dog were of great help, and cases were soon reported of the dog having spotted something in the darkness which would have gone unnoticed by an officer alone. One November evening on Mitcham Common, an officer was on patrol when his dog sensed the presence of two men in the darkness and led his handler to them. They were in possession of three sacks containing metal scrap stolen from a foundry nearby. Without the dog, the officer would have passed close by and been totally unaware of the men in hiding.

Soon after the experiment began, the grounds of Buckingham Palace were entered by a number of intruders, including two young American tourists, who had intended to sleep out in Hyde Park, found it inconveniently crowded, and climbed over the nearest wall, happily unaware that they were in the Palace gardens. Patrolling dogs enabled us to provide an additional safeguard for the Palace grounds and those of Clarence House. The dogs have proved equally useful in searching an area in which someone is believed to be hiding. A policeman heard unusual noises in the grounds of a convent, and in a short time Kim II, an Alsatian, found a man, who was arrested and charged with stealing four hundredweights of sheet metal, which he had hidden in the convent grounds.

The story of Rex III illustrates the value of the dog as a searcher in quite a different setting. About half-past four one morning a call was received from a large steel manufacturing plant, where three suspicious characters had just been seen to leave an office building. All available men were sent to the scene and began a search. As the premises covered a large area on the river bank, and it was easy to get into the adjoining buildings, a dog was called for. Rex III, an Alsatian, was sent with a handler and immediately began his search. Just before six o'clock a man was found by the dog, hidden in a remote part of the property, and at half-past seven, again with the aid of the dog, the other two men were discovered hiding on the roof of the premises next door.

Sometimes the capture is less important, as, for example, when the police were called to a garden to investigate rustling noises. They had searched for somone without any result until a dog led them at last to the cause of the suspicious rustling – a family of hedgehogs.

A few years ago there was an outbreak of bag-snatching in Hyde Park. The first warning would be a scream from the woman as the thief ran off, and even if a policeman was within earshot, the thief had too long a start. But his advantage ended with the arrival of the police dogs. It was not only speed that counted. The young thief, terror-stricken by the presence of a large dog, often threw up his hands and gave in as soon as he was overtaken.

A dog has proved to be more effective on many occasions than a number of policemen. One day a group of ten or a dozen young hooligans amused themselves by smashing up the chairs in Hyde Park and throwing them into the Serpentine. Two officers with their dogs approached the gang, who at once scattered in all directions. The officers alone could have done little about it; but Rajah and Earl rounded up the entire party and brought them in as quietly as a flock of sheep. Even more striking was the performance of a dog near Edgware. His handler saw five youths loitering near a group of parked cars and trying the door-handles. When he came up to question them, four ran away, but one showed fight. The dog soon quelled him, and was then sent after the other four. He rounded them up, brought them in to his master, and stood guard over all five outside a telephone kiosk while the officer called for a police van to take all his prisoners to the station.

We are still learning as we go and continually finding new uses for our dogs. We have trained handlers and dogs for a number of provincial and colonial police forces, and an interesting development has been the sending of Metropolitan-trained dogs to Malaya and Kenya. The fact that they have been trained to search and track without being held on a leash should make them specially valuable against terrorists who seek refuge in the jungle or the forest.

Perhaps the most important discovery we made in training was that our original idea of one man, one dog, was wrong. At first, each dog was taught to work on the command of only one man. By careful standardisation of the handlers' signs and words of command, however, it has proved possible to train some dogs to work with as many as six different handlers. The Labrador is the most satisfactory for this purpose, and works best for guard duties.

At first, many officers were sceptical of the dogs' usefulness, but as they got to work, calls for them became more and more frequent. The public, too, have been rapidly converted. Perhaps our most remarkable case was that of the dog called in at the tearful request of an old lady who had lost her tortoise, which had been forty years in the family. Given the scent from the tortoise's box, the dog followed it down the garden, through a hedge, across some allotments, and along a railway embankment to a group of brambles, where the missing tortoise was found asleep. Not strictly police work, no doubt, but very good for police prestige.

Chapter 19

THE PROBLEMS OF LONDON'S TRAFFIC

In 1952, 570 people were killed and 5,670 were seriously injured in the streets of London. The cost of traffic delays in London has been estimated at £70,000,000; and the London Transport Executive is of the opinion that an increase of only one mile an hour in the speed of the London bus would save the Executive £2,000,000 a year.

These striking figures summarise the heavy responsibility which control of London's traffic lays upon the Metropolitan Police. The police must reconcile two objects: to prevent accidents, and to keep the traffic moving. Before the war the figure of road casualties was steadily rising until, in 1938, 1,173 people were killed and 5,314 were seriously injured in London. The causes are analysed every year by the statistical department at Scotland Yard from detailed accident reports which are sent in every day by each division. This analysis shows clearly that the problem of accident prevention is far from being as simple as it is often represented to be, and that there is no single or universal remedy.

It is easy to blame the motorist and he is undoubtedly responsible in many cases. But not in all. The careless and inattentive pedestrian often acts in such a way that the motorist has no chance to avoid an accident. In too many cases, however, the fault does lie with motorists who may be unskilful, inattentive, careless or downright selfish. On the whole, it is not lack of skill but other factors which lead to accidents, and it is to these factors that the police direct their attention. They operate chiefly through the Traffic Patrols, a body of some 700 men using 100 cars and 145 motor-cycles.

In 1947, as an experiment, I decided to organise some of the Traffic Patrols in forty-eight Traffic and Accident Groups, each consisting of a car and two motor-cyclists available to be called at once by wireless to any point where there was a serious hold-up of traffic. This rapid concentration of trained officers where required has proved its value.

All Traffic Patrols are highly skilled drivers who have passed through the exacting tests of the Police Driving School. Two things are impressed on them: first, that their mission is to promote the full use and safety of the streets; and second, that their success will be measured not by the number of convictions they obtain, but by the extent to which their work leads to a reduction in accidents. Their objects are to set an example of safe and courteous driving; to assist and advise other road users to do the same; to admonish rather than to prosecute wherever possible; and in the last resort, to report for consideration any actual breaches of the law. It is little realised how few cases are taken to court. In 1951, over half a million verbal warnings were given on the spot; over 80,000 offences which were reported were dealt with by a written warning; and only 96,629 charges were made.

Prosecutions for speeding excite criticism, and it is frequently said that the police would be better employed in preventing crime than in harrying the motorist. But the patrols only concentrate on speeding on roads which the accident maps show to have a bad record; and, since deaths on the roads are at least ten times as many as deaths by murder or manslaughter, it seems to me unarguable that the traffic patrols are carrying out a primary duty – the protection of life. Most of the work is done by the patrol in a car or on a motor-cycle, using a carefully tested speedometer.

From time to time, spectacular work is done by the motor-cycle patrols. One of their best efforts was at Epsom Downs in 1952, when a young horse shied near the starting-post, threw his rider, leaped the rails and bolted across the Downs towards Tattenham Corner. He was followed by a police motor-cyclist who overtook him, grabbed the reins, and eventually brought him to a standstill after an exciting chase along a road busy with cars.

A more satisfactory achievement, for which traffic patrols must take much of the credit, is that, in spite of increased traffic, accidents are still well below the pre-war level. There were ninety fewer fatal accidents in 1952 than in the previous year. The patrols, operating in all weathers, have an arduous and sometimes dangerous task. Since the war, several motor-cyclist patrols have been killed, and many others have suffered serious injury.

Police work alone, however, can never wholly solve the

accident problem. It must be accompanied by a determined campaign of education and propaganda designed to make all road users conscious of the dangers, and of the need for care and safety. The police have taken a very active part in this campaign, in co-operation with the Royal Society for the Prevention of Accidents. By lecturers in schools and demonstrations in parks and school playgrounds, they have tried to teach successive generations of London children the principles of road safety, and thanks largely to their work, the children set a good example to many of their elders.

When I examined the statistics of accidents to children, I was impressed by the number which occurred when they were crossing the roads near their schools. In Middlesex, the County Council had organised, with good results, a system of adult patrols to control crossings near the schools. I tried to persuade other local authorities to do the same, but, with some laudable exceptions, they would not. Some, indeed, withdrew their patrols in case they might be held liable for damages if an error of judgement by the patrol should result in the injury or death of the children.

Finance was also a stumbling-block: should the grant be paid by the Ministry of Education or the Ministry of Transport? As in any event the local authorities pay half the cost of the police in London, the financial argument did not seem to me to be of great importance. At last, despairing of obtaining agreement, and concerned more with the safety of the children than with finance, I offered to undertake the organisation and training of patrols for the whole Metropolitan Police District, and this was eventually agreed. The number of school-crossing patrols was originally fixed at 1,050, and I had no difficulty in recruiting and training this number in a few months. The scheme has worked smoothly and well, and the number has now been increased to 1,400. These patrols are local men and women who undertake for a modest wage to attend at the school crossings four times a day, clothed in a white coat and carrying a board bearing the words 'Metropolitan Police. Children Crossing'. A Ministry of Transport regulation makes it an offence to ignore the patrols, which have undoubtedly saved many lives.

The police must also constantly study road conditions which make accidents likely. The Finchley Road, for instance, had a bad record until, as a result of representations by the police, a less skiddy material was laid down. There was an immediate reduction in the number of accidents. A few years ago I noticed that the refuges in the middle of the High Road at Tottenham were so frequent as to be dangerous to motorists. An analysis showed that the accident rate had, in fact, gone up since the refuges were installed. When we pointed this out, the number of refuges was reduced, and the accident rate went down again.

Meanwhile, as more and more cars come into use, our streets become more like car parks every day, and a reduced police force must continue to grapple with the problems of keeping the traffic moving. In September, 1951, the London Traffic Advisory Committee made a detailed survey which showed that in an area of about seven square miles of central London, including the City, some 25,000 cars were parked in the streets at about midday, nearly two-thirds of them for over two hours. During the whole business day from half-past nine in the morning to half-past five in the evening, the numbers were very little less. This gives some idea of the size of the problem. The law makes obstruction an offence, and constant efforts are made by the police to enforce the law. But shortage of men makes it impossible to do more than select particular streets and particular times for attention, with the result that motorists complain that they are harried one day in places where the day before they were left in peace. And knowing motorists' difficulties, magistrates can hardly fail to be sympathetic.

The one-way street has done a lot to ease the flow of traffic. So has the no-waiting rule, first applied to a number of 'yellow band' streets in the centre of London in June, 1947, and extended to the suburbs in November, 1948. Observation from the air before and after this rule was introduced showed that the speed of traffic in the main arteries had improved by a tenth; but lack of police has made regular enforcement impossible, and the gain is gradually being lost.

Unilateral parking has long been allowed in provincial cities and I urged its adoption in London as far back as 1947; but opposition by local authorities and traders delayed its introduction. At my urgent request, the scheme has been made to apply during the same hours as the no-waiting restrictions, since different hours would confuse motorists and make enforcement more difficult. There is no hope of changing most of the narrow streets of central London, and it is absurd to allow them to be blocked by rows of parked cars. The objections of shopkeepers are understandable, but their needs can be met by reasonable relaxations allowing vans to load or unload goods; and a trader is no more likely to lose customers because of a unilateral parking rule than because his street is blocked on both sides and in the middle by cars allowed to stop and go as they please.

When every use has been made of such schemes as one-way traffic, no parking and so on, the problem of the 25,000 vehicles standing in the streets will remain. Space for parking in or under new buildings is unlikely to make much difference for many years, and other places must therefore be found. Car parks at ground level would be prohibitively expensive in central London, even if open spaces were available.

We are left, therefore, with the idea of underground garages beneath squares and open spaces, or multi-storied garages partly above and partly below ground. Many squares and open spaces are ruled out because they are too small or of unsuitable shape, because of the disturbance to sewers, underground railways or other obstructions, or because there is no urgent parking problem in the area. A Ministry of Transport working party, after investigating the problems involved, selected nine London squares under which garages could be built to accommodate 3,540 cars at a total cost of £3,030,000. A similar survey into the possibility of garages above ground estimated that accommodation could be provided for 7,250 cars at a cost of £8,660,000.

The truth is that our streets have not kept pace with the immense growth of traffic, which has more than doubled in the last twenty years. The effect of even comparatively small improvements was illustrated in 1951, the year of the Festival of Britain, when on my urgent representations new roundabouts were constructed south of Waterloo Bridge and Westminster Bridge, and Parliament Square was reconstructed and enlarged. During the Festival, the severe hold-ups which we feared around the South Bank site were avoided, and ever since there has been a greatly improved flow of traffic in all three places.

We need new roads to allow traffic going east and west or north and south to get across central London without blocking the main arteries. Various plans have been drawn up, examined and pigeon-holed, and it would serve no useful purpose to examine them again here. It is not plans, but a decision to put plans into operation that is needed, and there can be no doubt that heavy as the cost would be, it would be amply repaid by saving time in almost every aspect of London life. The alternative is a creeping paralysis which in the end must prove fatal.

Chapter 20
GREET OCCASIONS

GREAT OCCASIONS

My first mounted appearance as Commissioner was at the State Opening of Parliament in 1945, which was also VJ-Day. In my two months at Scotland Yard I had been too busy to bother about riding practice, and I felt very lonely as I rode out into Whitehall, with thousands of eyes upon me, for my first mounted inspection. But Norton, who carried me on so many great occasions, behaved as a gentleman should, and as we rode back among the swarming crowds after the King's return to Buckingham Palace, I felt the worst was over and it could never be so bad again.

Since then there have been royal visits to St Paul's and Guildhall, visits of foreign sovereigns and heads of States, the marriage of Princess Elizabeth and Prince Philip, the funeral of King George VI, and finally the Coronation Procession of Queen Elizabeth II, when I rode with the G.O.C. London District immediately in front of the State Coach. Events of this kind demand long and detailed preparation, of which the Metropolitan Police have had more than a century's experience. The work is shared by two departments, that of Assistant Commissioner 'A', who is in charge of all the police on duty and responsible for keeping the route, and that of Assistant Commissioner 'B', who is responsible for organising the traffic so as to cause the least possible interference with the Londoner's routine.

Planning for the Coronation began a year beforehand, and I remember very clearly the first meeting of the Coronation Committee in an ice-cold room at St James's Palace. The Earl Marshal, the Duke of Norfolk, was our chairman. Some point cropped up on which no one seemed capable of taking a decision, and the hereditary Earl Marshal remarked dryly, 'I suppose I'd better undertake the responsibility. If I get the sack, it'll save me a lot of trouble.'

We all had occasion to feel like that during the ensuing twelve months. First of all, Major Margetson, the Assistant

181

Commissioner 'A', and his staff were asked to advise on the merits and difficulties of possible routes, and when this was settled they made a detailed survey of the streets through which the procession would pass.

Rehearsals of the Royal procession were held early on Sunday mornings, when there was no traffic, to see how long the journey would take and where corners or street refuges might need to be altered or removed to give free passage to the troops and the royal coach. Past experience had shown that at certain places, especially where there was even a gentle slope, the pressure of the crowd was liable to force spectators on to the route, despite the efforts of troops and police to hold the line. At the funeral of King George V, crowds at Hyde Park Corner and Marble Arch had almost brought the procession to a standstill. When he was briefing his officers on the arrangements for the funeral of King George VI, Major Margetson displayed photographs showing this breaking of the line, with the caption: 'This must never happen again.' With the aid of many miles of tubular steel guard rails, and some 2,000 men from the provincial police forces, the problem was solved, and photographs taken at the same places on the day of King George VI's funeral showed how successful the police arrangements had been.

With this experience in mind, 'A' Department examined the whole Coronation route, and at every corner or other danger point sockets were fixed during the winter, ready to take guard rails on Coronation Day. Other sockets were arranged to provide gangways through the crowds, so that people could cross the route up to the last moment. In all, seven miles of tubular steel rails were erected. A further safety measure was the erection of sixty-eight wooden barriers and gates, each nine feet high, across the streets leading to the route, so that when a particular section was full, any further influx of spectators, which would lead to dangerous overcrowding, could be cut off. With the same object, arrangements were made for Underground stations on the route to be closed at the request of a senior police officer when the size of the crowd made it necessary.

When all these physical barriers had been provided, 'A' Department had to consider the best arrangements for policing the route. With our depleted strength, it was obviously impossible to collect enough men for the entire route, and help had to be sought elsewhere. Our first reinforcement came from the Metropolitan Special Constables who, though only 3,000 strong, turned out 1,500 men on Coronation Day and many hundreds on the days that followed. Then, as always, the Commissioner of Police for the City of London came to our assistance and lent us several hundred men. Even so, the numbers were still insufficient, and arrangements were made to borrow 5,000 men from County and Borough forces. Every force was represented roughly in proportion to its size, and the men from each of the eight Police Districts in England and Wales were placed under the command of a senior officer of the district, through whom liaison was made with the Metropolitan Police. We also had the help of the military and naval police and the London Civil Defence Corps. In addition, the route was lined by some 2,500 men from the Navy, Army and Air Force. There were altogether some 16,000 police and 2,200 special constables along the route on Coronation Day.

As soon as the number of police available was known, 'A' Department drew up a detailed Operation Order setting out their duties: some to keep the line, cordon off side-streets or keep corridors open, others to preserve order behind the line and prevent people climbing on to dangerous structures, and so on. For each sector there was a reserve of men placed at a convenient point nearby, to reinforce those in the line whenever necessary, and in addition a general reserve at the disposal of the Assistant Commissioner was distributed at five points along the route.

For the first time, the women police were given responsibility for a complete sector, and were placed on the Victoria Embankment, where over 30,000 schoolchildren were to assemble to see the procession. Mounted Police were allotted in small numbers to the various sectors, and shortly before the procession started, a party of mounted men rode along the route ready to detach a few men at any points where help might be needed. Behind and among the crowds, C.I.D. officers in plain clothes were on duty to deal with crime and keep a look-out for any dangerous characters.

In a big operation of this kind, good communications are essential. Sixteen police vans and cars equipped with two-way wireless, and thirty-two motor-cycles, some with public address equipment, others with radio, were posted at intervals along the route, in touch with five fixed radio stations. Outside the processional areas a number of wireless cars were posted at selected points to control traffic and deal with the problems caused by its stoppage during the processions, and afterwards by its release.

The traffic problems were the concern of Mr Henry Dalton, Assistant Commissioner 'B'. His department's first task was to decide what streets must be closed to traffic, what diversions would be necessary as a result, and what streets must become temporarily one-way streets. Alterations in the routes and stopping-places of buses were discussed and agreed with London Transport, and it was decided to exclude motor coaches from the central area during Coronation week.

There remained one other problem for which past experience provided a warning rather than a model: the arrival and departure of the seven thousand people attending the Coronation ceremony in Westminster Abbey. At the Coronation of King George VI in 1937, the arrivals went according to plan, but the departures did not. It was impossible to get the large number of cars up to the exits from the Abbey, and this led to great delay. Guests became impatient and declined to wait their turn, and finally a steady downpour of rain led to confusion. Peers and peeresses in their robes were seen splashing through the puddles in a vain effort to find their cars, and many did not get away until late in the evening, having spent over twelve hours in the Abbey.

I was determined that on this occasion we would do better, and the marriage of Her Majesty, then Princess Elizabeth, had already given us the opportunity to try out new methods. Using our wireless communications and a system of labelling, it was possible to call cars up as they were needed. The results were very satisfactory, and the guests were able to leave within twenty minutes after the ceremony. For the Coronation I proposed to use the same methods, but to spread the taking-up over a much wider perimeter. The plan allowed guests to disperse on foot under covered ways to the Palace of Westminster and other buildings near the Abbey which could be more easily reached by cars, and where they could get food and refreshment while they waited.

In spite of the rain on Coronation Day, the plan worked well. The four thousand cars conveying guests to the Abbey drove in steadily by the appointed route, and only ten minutes after eight a.m., everyone was in. The arrangements for leaving worked equally well, and shortly after five o'clock the last car had been called up and the guests had left. There was, I believe, one car which did not come forward when called, owing to the fact that its chauffeur had been patriotically celebrating the occasion. The police, however, were able to cope with the situation. A motor-cycle patrol was despatched at top speed up Whitehall and along the Strand, with orders to return with a taxi. He found one outside the Savoy Hotel, and said to the driver, in the best traditions of detective fiction, 'Follow me'. A no doubt apprehensive taxi-driver was led through the crowds to the Abbey, and the waiting guest went on his way without undue inconvenience.

The night before the Coronation, I walked along part of the route. Already, at eleven p.m., in the drizzle, the patient crowds were in position, showing the enthusiasm, the good behaviour and ability to take care of themselves that they always do. They looked after anyone taken ill, and, when the moment came, handed out children to the front, so that the smallest could see. There was practically no crime on Coronation Day, and it was characteristic that when the police came on duty at half-past five in the morning, to line the route, they were greeted with a London cheer.

Of the day itself I have many memories. There was the deafening cheer that greeted the procession as we turned out of Northumberland Avenue into the Embankment, where 30,000 schoolchildren seemed determined to out-shout each other. There was a champagne lunch provided in a marquee for gold staff officers and other guests and which, as no one else came forward, I enjoyed almost alone. On the return journey, the air marshals' carriage made heavy going up St James's Street, and in tacking from side to side, lost its place, with the result that we passed four very disconsolate air marshals breasting the slope on foot. The Prime Minister's carriage broke down in Cockspur Street and failed to finish the course. At Marble Arch, the G.O.C., London District and I, immediately in front of the royal coach, came up with a military band which had broken prematurely into *God Save the Queen*, and was finishing the last few bars when it should have been beginning. The G.O.C., with a lack of respect for the National Anthem understandable in the circumstances, roared, 'Play that ruddy thing again!' and all was well.

When it was over, I rode back to Scotland Yard and had one of the most enjoyable hot baths of my life.

The police had a long and tiring day which did not finish with the returning procession, for in the evening thousands of people converged on Buckingham Palace and the Mall, or on the Victoria Embankment to see the firework display from the South Bank. Throughout the day, whether they were from London or the provinces, they had preserved their good humour and helpfulness. In commending their work Her Majesty voiced the opinion of everyone who had been in London on the day. One American visitor commented, 'The police were more like conductors with well-drilled orchestras than traffic cops. I didn't know traffic control could be perfect and painless.'

Another story came to me from the driver of the carriage for the popular Queen Salote of Tonga. On the way to the Abbey, when they were halted in the Mall, the driver noticed that one of the traces was broken, and was naturally afraid that if a second went, he would be unable to complete his journey. However, he consoled himself with the thought that it was an inside trace, and hoped for the best. While he was halted a second time in Trafalgar Square, a mounted police inspector asked him why he looked so worried. He explained his trouble, and the inspector asked, 'Will a chain be any use to you?'

'But where can you get a chain at this time in Trafalgar Square?' the coachman said, looking round at the several thousand people who filled the square.

The inspector dismounted, removed the bridle chain from his horse, and fitted it to the pole of the carriage. It finished its journey to and from the Abbey without further incident, and the crowds were able to enjoy the spectacle of that gracious and majestic lady braving the rain in the carriage which she so resolutely refused to have closed.

But even Coronation Day was not the end for the police, for in the next two weeks the enormous crowds of sightseers on foot, in cars and in motor coaches made it almost impossible to move in any of the decorated streets on the processional route. Twelve months before the Coronation, motor coach companies had been given permission to bring visitors to London provided they set them down outside the central area. The coaches came to London in thousands, and moved slowly along nose to tail in a never-ending stream. The unhappy Londoner going about his business or to and from work suffered uncomplainingly for a time, but then began to be restive. Members of Parliament, delayed in getting to the House, began to inquire what the Commissioner of Police was doing to carry out the Sessional Standing Order and keep the approaches of the Palace of Westminster free of obstruction.

I therefore made an order prohibiting coaches from entering the central area for two more weeks. By the end of that time the rush was over and London traffic returned to normal. There were some protests at the ban, but I suspect that the coach drivers were quite happy to see it imposed. One evening, during the worst of the crush, a motor coach drove into Scotland Yard itself and the driver asked where he was. On being told, he said, 'Ah've had enough. Ah want to go home to Lancasheer.'

The police could never have coped with these unprecedented crowds by the use of compulsion. It was their good humour and understanding of the British public, and the crowds' own cheery good sense, that made the situation bearable and even amusing. One night at about half-past ten I walked through Trafalgar Square, where cars and people covered every square yard of roadway. A young policeman was wrestling with the traffic. I asked him if the ban on coaches had made things easier.

'Yes, sir,' he said. 'I can manage the buses and the cars. You can tell them what to do, but you can't tell these thousands of foot passengers.'

It was true enough, and yet when I squeezed my way through the Admiralty Arch into the Mall, then a solid mass of people with hardly any cars, I found no disorder. The people had organised themselves. Those walking eastward towards Trafalgar Square were on the north side of the road, and those walking westward were on the south. As an exhibition of mass common sense it was remarkable, and explained why with so few policemen these great assemblies of people never seem to result in any serious incident.

'They're good people,' said a chief superintendent, looking paternally out of his car at the crowds along the routes of a Royal drive, which were controlled by one policeman to perhaps fifty yards. 'No trouble at all.'

By a curious chance, my official life began with the coronation of King George V and ended with that of his grand-daughter. When I passed the Civil Service examination in 1910, Mr Churchill, as he was then, was Home Secretary, and contrary to all established practice he insisted that before I was appointed to the Home Office he must see me. I came up rather nervously to be interviewed by this already legendary figure, who had just provided headlines by his presence at the Battle of Sidney Street and his endeavours to give another chance to the Dartmoor Shepherd, an elderly pilferer who had spent thirty-eight of his sixty-seven years in jail. I had the vaguest ideas about the work of a government department and it came as a surprise to be told how John Moylan, who later became Receiver of the Metropolitan Police District, had been despatched at short notice in Mr Churchill's fur coat to act as civil liaison officer with General Sir Nevil Macready in the force sent to deal with the disturbances at Tonypandy.

Mr Churchill put me through an interrogation which included the inquiry, 'Why have you chosen a sheltered life like that of a civil servant?'

I said, thinking of Moylan and Sidney Street, that it sounded a very interesting life, and this was a lucky reply.

'Yes, it is indeed,' said Mr Churchill, and for half an hour I listened spellbound to an impromptu discourse on the problems and art of administration.

Not many young civil servants can have had a similarly august introduction to their chosen career. A few weeks later, when I joined the Home Office, I spent some time examining and suggesting replies to loyal addresses on the coronation of King George V. Another subject with which I was at once concerned was the Metropolitan Police. One fact alone illustrates the change that has come over police administration in these years, largely as a result of the work of Sir Arthur Dixon who, from the end of the first world war until his retirement in 1946 was continuously in charge of police affairs at the Home Office. The department in which I served dealt with the Metropolitan Police, but we knew nothing of the provincial police, who were dealt with by an entirely separate department. It was Sir Arthur Dixon's great achievement to have raised police standards to a new level over the whole country and to have initiated in many fields advances in methods which have transformed police work out of all knowledge.

My own service began under Mr Churchill, and ended under Sir Winston. It covers forty-two years and I have enjoyed it all, but none more than my eight years with the Metropolitan Police. From them I received a loyalty and a friendship which I shall always treasure. Their capacity for organisation has to be seen at close quarters to be believed. I always knew that whether it was a state function or a criminal inquiry, a social event or a horse show, there would be no loose ends. Everything would be attended to in an orderly and intelligent sequence. At the Police College one night, a provincial officer greeted the Metropolitan contingent, who had just arrived with the words. 'Here come the Grand and Glorious.' Spoken part in jest, part in earnest, the words may well serve as an epilogue to my story.

The record of the Metropolitan Police is indeed grand and glorious. Commissioners come and go, but the Force remains to face the problems of an ever-changing world. In this century it has survived more than one attack on its competence and integrity, it has played a vital part in the defence of London in two great wars, and with only occasional and very limited emergency powers has preserved the peace, while leaving our essential liberties unimpaired. If it has not wholly achieved the professional status to which its aspires, it has made real progress towards it. It is significant that, whereas up to forty years ago the policeman and his Commissioner were the constant subject of Mr Punch's sly and not always friendly humour, they seldom appear in his pages today.

Trained not merely to enforce, but to observe the law, the policeman has long since lived down the hatred and ridicule to which his forerunners were subjected, and has gained for himself the respect and affection of all but a lawless minority. He serves the State regardless of the political complexion of the government of the day, and his impartial enforcement of the law has become the very cornerstone of our democratic way of life.

In our police forces the British people have a unique instrument which it is essential they should preserve. Successive governments have declared it as settled policy that the highest posts in the service should be filled by police officers, and in the appointment of my deputy, Sir John Nott-Bower, as my successor, this policy was reaffirmed at the highest level. This is all to the good, but the policy presupposes a supply of suitable men to fill these top posts. The Police College is doing a great work in preparing men already in the service for higher rank, but it can only deal with the material that is there. Unless this is of the right quality the College cannot succeed, and conditions in the police service must be good enough to attract young men of character and ability who intend to make the service their career and to fit themselves to rise to the top.

The service makes great demands on those who join it, and it cannot truthfully be said that the rewards it offers are even yet sufficient. I look forward to a time when the successful police officer, as a matter of course, will decide to encourage his son to enter the service as a military or naval officer encourages his son to enter the Army or Navy. That is not the case today, and before it can happen even greater changes than we have seen will have to be made.

Better pay, including adequate compensation for the additional cost of life in London, more houses and modern police stations must come first. I believe they would be followed by an increase in the numbers of the Force that would open the way to improvements in organisation which are today hindered by lack of men. More men would make it possible to reduce hours of duty and give some relief from work at night, at week-ends and during holidays, to develop fully the system of team policing, and to rearrange divisions and sub-divisions so as to give better cover to many places that now complain, with some cause, that they are not getting the police protection they need.

More men would allow of more time being spent on training. Each year the demands on the intelligence and the technical knowledge of the policeman grow greater, and it is already impossible to cram into the three months' probationer training all the things a policeman must know. More refresher courses at regular intervals during an officer's service, more general education courses for men in the middle years of their service, more opportunities to see something of the work of other forces at home and abroad, are all needed if the policeman of the future is to be competent to deal with an ever more complicated world.

Given these things, I have no doubt men will be found in the Force itself, capable of leading it to ever greater heights of public service.

Tough! Moving! Authentic!

Don Carpenter's
HARD RAIN FALLING   5/–

The powerful novel of two young criminals in
and out of prison; of their life and their
loving and their crimes, of their luck and the
way their luck runs out.
Strong meat. An incredibly successful blend of
detachment and compassion . . . an
uncomfortable reminder of the thin wall of
circumstance which separates most of us from
Jack Levitt and Billy Lancing.

'Written with authority, detachment and
almost uncanny deadpan intelligence . . .
compelling readability . . . an impressive
achievement . . . an important contribution to
modern fiction'
The Spectator